OVERVIEW

Overview

How do you go about finding the best possible person to fill a job? Although interviewing candidates is important, it can waste a lot of time – and be unproductive – if you don't have the right types of candidates to interview.

The key to both successful interviewing and hiring is effective screening. This involves filtering resumes to find job candidates who are best suited for the position.

What do you think happens if you don't screen applicants properly? You'll probably ignore some credible candidates who deserve an interview.

You'll also waste time on interviewing unsuitable candidates, who aren't qualified for the position you need to fill.

This course will help you avoid these pitfalls, ensuring that you identify the best possible applicants to include in the interviewing process.

The first step in screening

You might think the first step is weeding through job applications to identify the candidates who meet a basic set of requirements. But actually, the first step is creating an accurate job description for the position you need to fill. This is a vital part of the screening process. It ensures you know what you're searching for in the candidate you'll hire.

A good job description sets out the expectations for the job and for the candidate you'll ultimately hire.

Before you can write a good job description, you need to perform a job analysis. You examine what the job entails – for example, what skills and qualifications the person in this role needs and what tasks the new employee needs to perform to succeed in the role.

From this analysis, you create the job description, which accurately identifies all the requirements a successful candidate must meet.

An incomplete or inaccurate job description can be disastrous. For example, say you need to hire a graphic designer for your advertising agency. The job requires someone with experience in using a specific desktop publishing software product. If you fail to include this in the job description, you may hire someone unsuitable and end up having to spend time and money on training this person.

Once you've created an accurate job description and advertised the job, the next step is to screen applicants' resumes to determine who meets the job requirements.

At this point, your success in identifying suitable candidates for interviewing will depend on the accuracy of the requirements you included in your job description.

You should be able to quickly determine who meets the minimum job requirements you identified and weed out those that don't. Then you can examine more closely the remaining resumes.

You also need to screen resumes for red flags. These signal potential problems that could arise once an applicant is hired. Very frequent job changes, for example, might indicate that someone's unlikely to stick with the job for long.

In this book, you'll learn how best to conduct each of the three main steps involved in determining the right candidates to interview:
- performing a job analysis in which you identify all key job requirements, and then writing an accurate job description,
- screening resumes based on the job requirements and discarding those that don't meet specified criteria, and
- screening remaining resumes for any red flags.

For your organization to be effective, it needs to hire the best employees. So when you're interviewing candidates for a job, how do you go about choosing the best person? It's common for those who carry out interviews simply to rely on their gut feelings – but this can lead to costly mistakes.

Consequences of hiring mistakes

A bad judgment call during the hiring process can have significant negative consequences for an organization.

Someone lacking the skills and attributes to do a job properly is likely to require extra training and supervision, which can be expensive. This person may also make frequent mistakes, be unable to complete tasks – which must then be reassigned to other employees, fail to get along with other staff members, and even damage customers' perceptions of the organization.

Ultimately, a bad hiring choice can mean that an organization has to invest time and money in repeating the recruitment and hiring processes.

Typically, conducting job interviews is the final step you perform in the recruitment process. The interviews determine who you or your organization ultimately hires.

This means it's crucial to interview job candidates well.

Gut feelings may still have a role to play when it comes to choosing the best person for a job – but they're not enough. For interviews to be effective, interviewers must use a structured approach. They need to prepare adequately in advance and avoid a range of common errors that lead to judgment mistakes.

It's also important to be aware of the legal implications surrounding interviews. For example, asking questions that discriminate unfairly against candidates based on their age, gender, marital status, or religion is illegal. But interviewers may ask these types of questions without realizing the implications.

In this books, you'll learn the following essentials for preparing to interview:
- how best to prepare before conducting an interview,
- the five common errors interviewers make, so that you can avoid these when you're preparing for and conducting interviews, and
- the relevant legal issues, so you know what it is and isn't appropriate to include in interviews.

Effective interviews require consistency and reliability. If different interviewers get different impressions of the same candidates, something's wrong.

How to get the most out of your interviews

The way to get the most out of an interview is to follow a structured format. You start off by putting candidates at ease so you can get the best out of them, then ask clear, thorough, consistent questions of each candidate, and finally close the interview on a positive note.

If you have a format you can follow, you're less likely to leave out important questions and more likely to discover everything you need to know about the candidate. This helps ensure you hire the right person for the job.

Also, you'll prevent high turnover by ensuring you provide all the necessary information about the company and the available position to candidates. That way, employees won't be surprised by anything once they start the job.

In this book, you'll learn how to open an interview so that the candidate feels at ease and communicates openly with you. You'll also discover how to ask effective questions that are clear, thorough, and consistent, so you draw out all the information you need. Finally, you'll learn how to close an interview on a positive note, making sure you've covered everything.

Because part of the purpose of an interview is to help candidates decide whether they want to work for your organization, an effective interview should allow time for candidates to ask questions.

Also, remember that it's up to you, as a representative of your organization, to conduct yourself professionally during all phases of the interview process.

How do you determine who is the best candidate for the job? What if two candidates both have the experience and the technical skills needed for the role you're interviewing for?

Behavioral-based interviewing can help you make an effective decision about candidates. As well as investigating technical skills and experience, it involves examining the candidates' behavior. This can help you determine which candidate exhibits the behaviors required for success at the given job.

Behavioral-based interview questions ask candidates to explain how they behaved in response to previous situations - situations that are related to the competencies needed for the available job.

These types of questions are designed to elicit facts about candidates' past behavior, rather than general attitudes or opinions.

As such, they can help minimize bias in the interviewing process.

Behavioral-based interviewing isn't new – it has been used for decades. It's gaining in popularity though.

And this is because of its benefits. It provides a more accurate idea of the ideal candidate for a job, it gives insight into how candidates have dealt with real life situations, and it's a structured, objective approach.

In this book, you'll learn about the essentials of behavioral interview techniques:

- the definition of behavioral-based interviewing and this technique's benefits,
- how to develop questions for the behavioral-based interview, and
- how to use behavioral-based questions in practice.

Early in the hiring process, you develop a detailed job description that sets out the requirements for a job. Then you gather information about candidates through interviewing and testing. Now it's time to evaluate each candidate you interviewed so you can make a hiring decision.

The best way to go about evaluating candidates is to use a structured approach – reviewing how well their answers to interview questions reveal their readiness to take up the position. You want to evaluate and compare candidates in a way that's fair and consistent, using job-related criteria. In turn, this makes it more likely you'll make the best hiring decision.

Next you check the references of the candidate you've selected. This person's previous employers may have information that's vital you take into account.

Knowing how to check references effectively can improve your hiring decisions.

Once you know who's best suited to the available position, it's time to make this person a job offer.

This requires careful consideration. Remember, there's nothing to stop the candidate you've chosen from rejecting your offer. So the offer you make has to be attractive, as well as fair.

How you make the offer is also important because doing this is the basis for a legal employment contract.

Once the chosen candidate accepts a position, you might think the hiring process is over. But an important step remains – you need to inform all unsuccessful candidates of your decision. Failing to do this can reflect badly on your company.

In this book, you'll learn how to evaluate candidates once you've completed interviews, how to check their references effectively, and how best to make an offer to the candidate you select. This will equip you to secure the best possible candidate for a job.

CHAPTER I - SCREENING APPLICANTS FOR INTERVIEWING

CHAPTER I - Screening Applicants for Interviewing

In this chapter, you'll learn how best to conduct each of the three main steps involved in determining the right candidates to interview:
- performing a job analysis in which you identify all key job requirements, and then writing an accurate job description,
- screening resumes based on the job requirements and discarding those that don't meet specified criteria, and
- screening remaining resumes for any red flags.

KEY COMPONENTS OF A GOOD JOB DESCRIPTION

Key components of a good job description

The basis of a job description
Many employees have never been given written descriptions of their jobs. Their companies might not provide these due to simple oversight, indiscriminate hiring during growth periods, or the perceived flexibility it gives them not to codify job responsibilities. But this is unfortunate, because job descriptions have important functions.

Purpose of job descriptions
A job description should define what a job entails – the reason why the job exists, how it fits into the company structure, the main responsibilities associated with it, and how success in the job is measured.

Before you start work on a job description for an available position, something to consider is whether the position is actually necessary. Many companies hire new employees based on vaguely defined needs, only to find themselves overstaffed with potentially confused employees.

So you begin by asking yourself some questions. For example, what's the purpose of the job? Who currently does the job? How long has the position existed or is it a new position? How much will the position cost the company? And finally, will the position still exist in two years?

Once you're certain there's a job to fill, you need to analyze the requirements for that job carefully. This ensures you hire the right person for the job.

When a job analysis is required, it's preferable to have an objective manager or even external consultant do it, rather than the person currently doing the job. This is because a current jobholder might try to inflate the importance or responsibility of the position.

To perform an effective analysis of a position, you need to determine several factors:

- who the direct manager is for the position,
- the specific tasks that the job requires *(These tasks can be divided into "primary duties" and "secondary duties" on the job analysis form.)*,
- who the person in the position will need to supervise – whether internal or external to the company the required training and qualifications *(This includes the education level needed for the position.)*, and
- the required experience and skills.

See below each section of the job analysis form to find out how it feeds into an accurate job analysis.

Primary and secondary duties:

The specific tasks required are the meat and potatoes of the job – the tasks the employee will perform each day. It can be useful to divide these into primary and secondary duties on an analysis form, to indicate the relative priorities of the different tasks.

For example, the primary duties for a content editor position might include: 1. Edit articles and columns to make sure they conform to house style and maintain a high standard of grammar, 2. Liaise with journalists and other editorial staff to make sure submitted content conforms to house style and is grammatically sound, 3. Follow in-house uploading and admin processes to ensure that content is edited and uploaded by deadline, and 4. Report to the editor and carry out team tasks and processes when required. Secondary duties include 1. Research and write articles when needed, 2. Participate in marketing drives by coordinating with Marketing and preparing related material, and 3. Keep records of submissions and publication dates.

Direct manager:

The direct manager is the person directly above the position you need to fill in the company structure. This person is likely to have useful input for the job analysis.

The content editor position's direct manager is the editor.

Supervises (position/s in company):

As part of your analysis, you should list anyone the successful candidate will supervise, as well as those in more senior positions and external partners or customers. Including this information can help clarify what expectations the person who fills the position must meet, as well as how the position fits into your company's overall structure and processes.

The content editor position 1. Coordinates in-house journalists and freelancers.

Specific training and education level needed:

It's essential to determine the minimum level of education and any specialized training required for the position. You should do this based on the tasks and specific responsibilities associated with the job.

The specific training needed for the content editor position is 1. Computer literacy, 2. Knowledge of HTML and web publishing software, and 3. Knowledge of word processing and layout software. The Education level needed is an undergraduate degree in journalism, communications, or related field.

Experience and skills:

As well as identifying required qualifications, your analysis should identify the skills and experience required to do the job. It's important to be specific when detailing the required skills. A general description like "good communication skills," for example, is too vague. Is it that the position requires someone able to write clear, accurate reports for management? Or does the position require good public-speaking skills?

For example, the experience and skills needed for the content editor position include 1. Three to five years editing experience in an online environment, 2. Writing to brief, 3. Writing to a house style, 4. Proofreading, 5. Good knowledge of web-based content management systems, 6. Good interpersonal communication skills, 7. Good time management, and 8. Good attention to detail.

Your job analysis should also describe the resources required to perform the job duties. It can cover everything from the tools needed – such as a computer or specialized equipment – to funds for sending a person on business trips.

It's also vitally important to assess how much time is required to fulfill the job duties. Can they be completed within full, normal work hours? This will make it clear whether you need to hire multiple employees, a single full-time person, or someone to work part time.

You may also want to describe methods of measuring job performance in your analysis. Determining this as part of a job analysis can help clarify what will be expected of the employee, as well as paving the way for valid, objective performance appraisals.

The descriptions in an analysis should be as detailed and measurable as possible, to give a clear picture of what the job actually entails. Take the example of primary duties listed on the job analysis for a content editor.

The more specific the description, the more likely it is that suitable candidates will apply for the position.

Once you've completed a thorough job analysis, you're in a position to create an accurate job description.

A good job description should include four key components:
- a brief overview of the position, including the job title,
- how the position fits into the reporting structure,
- a list of the tasks and responsibilities associated with the job, and
- the qualifications and skills required for the position.

Some wonder whether the compensation for the job should be included in the job description.

It's recommended that you avoid setting a level of compensation on a job description, because this changes regularly due to market fluctuations and other factors.

Overview of the position

When writing an overview for a job description, you should be clear and concise about what the job entails. You may use this description for the advertisement you'll publish in a newspaper or online to attract response to an open position.

In the job description's overview section, you provide a succinct description of the primary reason for the job and the main responsibilities associated with it. The primary and secondary duties you identified in a job analysis inform your wording of this description.

You use action verbs to describe the main purpose and duties of the job in the overview. In the example of a content editor's job description, you would state that this person's tasks are to edit, prepare, and write content, and maintain records.

You shouldn't begin your description with a question, especially one that's loaded. Your overview should get to the point – rather than ask rhetorical questions or include marketing cliches.

Remember, this document will help you screen applicants and formulate interview questions.

Question

Which job overviews successfully convey the function and duties of the given positions?

Options:

1. Grants officer – Reviews grant applications to make sure they meet organizational requirements. Contacts and advises applicants regarding grants. Maintains records of applications.

2. Nursery assistant – Assists in the function of nursery as a safe, stable, and stimulating place of care for children.

Encourages children to play educational games and read. Keeps the nursery clean.

3. Secretary – Typing, paperwork, and filing. Phones. Administrative tasks.

4. Sales manager – Seeking a self motivated marketing machine who is going for gold. Will motivate the team to blow their targets right out of the water and put this company on the map.

Answer:

Option 1: This option is correct. This overview lists the main functions and duties associated with the position.

Option 2: This is a correct option. This overview lists the main duties of the position, providing a succinct description of what the job entails.

Option 3: This option is incorrect. The descriptions of the duties provided in this overview are too general and don't give potential applicants any real grasp of what the position will entail. It also doesn't use action verbs, so it's difficult to follow.

Option 4: This is an incorrect option. This overview sounds more like a marketing blurb. It doesn't provide a summary of what the job entails. It won't be very useful as a guide for screening candidates.

Reporting structure

The reporting structure section of a job description explains where the position is situated in the company hierarchy and which other employees the successful candidate will interact with. From this, you should be able to tell who supervises the position and who this position supervises.

You take the information about who supervises whom from the job analysis form to define the reporting structure in the job description. Adding this information to the job description gives you the context of the position in the organization.

The job description for the content editor position, for example, specifies that the position is part of the Editing Department. It also specifies that the job holder will report directly to the editor, and liaise with journalists and freelance content producers regarding content.

An accurate picture of the reporting structure will help to ensure you get the best applicants for the job.

It's important to include this information because understanding how the position fits in the organizational structure may be a deciding factor in whether your favored candidates will consider the position or not.

You need to know how new hires will interact with other employees and what the job means to the progress of the company. Then when it comes time to interview, you can provide candidates with a clear description of the reporting structures.

Question

Which example provides the most effective description of the reporting structure for the position of associate editor?

Options:

1. This position reports directly to the editor, who in turn reports to the managing director. The director oversees all of the departments, with managers from each reporting to the director.

2. The person in this position reports to the editor and will carry out various writing assignments, in addition to administrative tasks.

3. This position reports to the editor and acts as a facilitator, as well as the primary liaison, between authors, reviewers, and editors in pre-production project development and during the production and marketing phases of projects.

Answer:

Option 1: This option is incorrect. It mentions the position's direct superior, but then focuses too much on the managing director's place in the organization.

Option 2: This option is incorrect. Although this description says who the position reports to, it doesn't clarify further how the associate editor fits in the organization – how the person will interact with other employees and what the job means to the progress of the company.

Option 3: This is the correct option. It articulates how the position fits in the organization and who the person in the position will need to interact with.

List of responsibilities

Drawing on the results of the job analysis, the job description lists relevant responsibilities and duties in order of importance. These tasks should clearly meet the company's needs and not replicate the duties that someone working in another position already fulfills. For example, the most important duty of a content editor is to edit content so it meets standards for publication on the site.

So you should avoid modeling the list of responsibilities on those of a previous job holder. Employees have their own slant on priorities and their own approach to a job.

If the job description outlines what the company needs rather than what someone else is currently doing in the role, the interviewers have a better chance of finding the candidate who can carry out the job to the organization's expectations.

When writing the lists of tasks, you should avoid too much detail on too many responsibilities, because this can be confusing. You need to stick to the major responsibilities, explaining them clearly and succinctly.

And even if the job in question is highly technical, try to avoid using acronyms and obscure terminology – which not everyone will understand. In addition, eliminate biased terminology by creating sentences for which gender pronouns are not required.

Finally, don't use subjective modifiers or words that might lead to misinterpretations – for example, words like "sometimes," "several," or "high level."

In the case of the content editor description, the tasks listed correspond to the major responsibilities.

There is just enough detail provided to give a reasonable idea of what the job will entail in the day to day work environment.

Throughout a job description – but especially when listing responsibilities – it's best to stick to short, simple sentences, which are easy to understand.

Start with an action verb and try to be as specific as you can. Avoid vague verbs like "produce," "perform," or "assist" unless you clarify them by asking yourself who, what, when, how often, and who else is involved when performing an action, for example.

For example, the verb "performs" in "performs team admin" is vague and needs more explanation. Rewriting it as "Administers team leave and overtime records" clarifies what this task involves.

In the example of the content editor's responsibilities, the list is informative yet brief. You can be specific without being overly wordy if you select the right words to convey what needs to be done.

Question

Which of the tasks for the job description of assembly line supervisor are effectively written?

Options:

1. Keeps staff time-sheets up to date, and maintains records of leave and sick leave

2. Oversees printing of EEC forms

3. Resets conveyor belt settings when unexpected jams occur

4. Types weekly status reports for the manager, to be forwarded to other managers in the region, who will then collate data on status

Answer

Option 1: This option is correct. A well-written list of tasks and responsibilities contains items that clearly describe the required task without going into unnecessary detail.

Option 2: This option is incorrect. The verb "oversee" is vague and isn't followed with explanation that makes it clear what this task involves. In addition, the task description includes an acronym, which may not be clear to everyone.

Option 3: This option is correct. The task is presented in an easy to understand way, with little room for incorrect interpretation.

Option 4: This option is incorrect. The actual task is the typing of weekly reports. The additional information is completely extraneous.

Skills and qualifications

The final section of a good job description is a list of required qualifications and skills. These are determined by the skills needed to perform the primary duties outlined in the job analysis form. You can only specify needed skills, attributes, or credentials when you know what tasks the job holder will be responsible for.

This list should contain all requirements in relation to these areas:

- **education level** - For example, "undergraduate degree in journalism, communications, or a related field".
- **work experience** - For example, "three to five years editing experience in an online environment".
- **specialized knowledge**, and - For example, "in-depth knowledge in web-based content management systems".
- **assortment of essential skills** - For example, "excellent proofreading, good interpersonal, and good time management skills, as well as good attention to details".

Any specialized knowledge needed for the position should also be detailed in this section, including knowledge of equipment, procedures, or standards. The knowledge requirements dictate what is needed before an employee can start actually doing the job. In the example of the content editor, the person filling the position needs to know how to use the web-based content management system.

It's a bad idea to inflate the required qualifications and skills. Although it might seem to make sense to canvass for job candidates with the most impressive lists of qualifications, this can be counterproductive.

Unnecessary requirements

If a qualification like a degree isn't necessary for the job, setting it as a requirement may prevent a large number of potentially suitable candidates from applying for the job. It can also mislead candidates – both those who apply and those who don't – about what the job entails and requires. Moreover, those who screen resumes may weed out perfectly suitable candidates.

It's important to avoid including job requirements that discriminate unfairly against candidates based on criteria like age, physical ability, or gender.

For example, requiring that only candidates under the age of 35 apply for a position constitutes discrimination unless there's a legitimate reason why someone older couldn't perform the relevant job.

Once you have a draft of your job description ready, you should have other people review it for accuracy and ease of comprehension.

You should compare the job description to the analysis on which it's based to pick up any errors or misleading statements.

Case Study: Question 1 of 2
Scenario

As the HR manager at a financial services company, you need to recruit a new librarian. You've completed a comprehensive job analysis with input from the current head librarian and have drafted a job description for the position.

Question

Which key components of good job descriptions are included in the example description?

Options:

1. Overview
2. Reporting structure
3. Task and responsibilities
4. Qualifications and skills

Answer:

Option 1: This option is correct. The overview details the functions of the job without going into too much detail.

Option 2: This option is incorrect. The description doesn't mention the reporting structure. According to the analysis, the librarian reports to the chief information officer and trains all staff, and also supervises an assistant librarian.

Option 3: This option is correct. The description lists the primary tasks for the role in section 2, including preparing research reports and verifying facts.

Option 4: This option is correct. The qualifications and skills for the job are listed in section 3. These include a postgraduate diploma in library and information science and three years experience in an information management position.

Case Study: Question 2 of 2

Which component is not presented effectively in this example of a job description?

Options:

1. Overview, because it leaves out parts of the job described in the job analysis

2. Tasks and responsibilities, because it doesn't list all the vital information contained in the job analysis

3. Qualifications and skills, because it fails to include all the qualifications and skills listed in the job analysis

Answer:

Option 1: This option is incorrect. The overview in the job description is appropriate. It identifies the primary duties and function of the job.

Option 2: This option is incorrect. All the main responsibilities of the position are specific and clear.

Option 3: This is the correct option. The job analysis includes the requirement that the person have online information management skills and verbal and written communication skills. These are missing from the job description.

An accurate job description helps to ensure a common understanding of what a job will entail and makes screening potential candidates more effective.

A job description should be based on the results of a thorough job analysis. Its key components should include an overview outlining the main responsibilities and duties of the job, the reporting structure associated with the job, a clear, ordered list of the prospective job holder's responsibilities, and a list of necessary qualifications and skills.

TECHNIQUES FOR SCREENING RESUMES

Techniques for screening resumes

Resumes and application forms

It's common to receive a large volume of resumes for a job you advertise. But many of the applicants may be unsuitable or unqualified for the position. So what's an efficient way to weed out mismatched candidates and find those who are really worth following up on?

The answer is to screen your applicants using the job description you have created for the open position. This helps you identify the candidates who are worth interviewing for the position.

Doing this saves time and effort, because it simply doesn't make sense to interview applicants who don't meet the basic requirements for a job.

When you advertise a job, you can ask prospective candidates to submit an application form or send in a resume. In some cases, you may want to ask for both.

The two formats differ in areas such as presentation style and ease of use, and are generally suitable for different job types.

See each area in which resumes and application forms differ to learn more about it.

Presentation style

A resume format gives applicants the freedom to present information using the layouts they prefer, rather than a prescribed structure. This enables applicants to be creative in their presentation – an attribute that may be important for the position they're applying for.

An application form requires applicants to present information in a prescribed format.

Ease of use

In a resume, it can be difficult to find the information you need quickly. Because an application form uses a predefined layout, it makes it much easier to find relevant information and to compare different applicants' details.

Job type

Traditionally, resumes are requested for skilled or professional positions, and application forms are used for nonprofessional positions – or those requiring unskilled or semi-skilled labor.

Each format has both advantages and disadvantages.

For example, resumes allow applicants to provide highly specific information about themselves – information that can be difficult to illicit in an application form. However, they may also leave out important information that an application form asks for.

With an application form, you can specifically request particular information. And if a section in the form is left blank, it can alert you to a potential issue with the applicant. However, you may get a less rounded picture of the applicant than you would via a resume.

In the end, you need to assess your needs and decide which format – resume or application form – is the most suitable for the position you need to fill.

The focus of this topic is on screening resumes.

The resume screening process

Whenever you screen resumes for a position, you should keep the job description for the position in front of you.

This is because you need to assess applicants' resumes against the exact requirements for the job – which should be clearly outlined in the job description.

It's important to make a conscious effort to focus on the predetermined job requirements. For example, avoid letting unrelated criteria – like creativity in presentation – influence your assessment.

To help you screen resumes, keep these three questions in mind:

- What are the prerequisites for the position?
- Are there any special requirements in your organization?
- Which qualifications are key for success in the role?

Different organizations use different processes to screen resumes – and different processes may even be used within the same organization for different jobs. For efficiency though, any resume screening process should typically be broken down into two basic steps – a quick overview, followed by more detailed screening.

See each step to find out what it entails.

1. Quick overview

A quick overview gives you a general idea of the applicants. In this step, you skim all the resumes and remove those from applicants who are clearly unsuitable.

2. Detailed screening

During detailed screening, you go through each resume in depth, assessing specific attributes to distinguish the best applicants. Your aim at this stage should be to narrow the pool of applicants down to a shortlist of potential candidates, who you'll then call in for interviews.

In the quick overview stage, you pick one or two essential, quantifiable attributes required of the successful job candidate, and then review each resume, checking for these attributes.

For example, a major job requirement could be two years of experience in a similar position plus local government-certified training. During a quick overview, you can immediately remove the resumes of all applicants who don't meet these requirements.

During the detailed screening stage, you focus on specific knowledge, experience, and qualifications that are needed for the job.

For example, your freight transport company requires a business analyst to work on an electronic tracking system. The successful applicant may require in-depth knowledge of road transport systems, five years' experience in a transport logistics environment, an advanced degree in information systems, and a professional certification in business analysis.

In your detailed screening, you'd analyze each resume, searching for the applicants who meet or surpass the specified requirements.

However, bear in mind that you may need to balance requirements. For example, applicants' professional experience may outweigh the importance of their educational qualifications. One applicant may have a postgraduate degree and five years experience. Another applicant with only an undergraduate degree may be a better choice, if this person happens to have 20 years of experience in the relevant industry.

Two other aspects to consider carefully are career goals and achievements. See each aspect to find out why it's important.

Career goals

It's best to consider applicants whose career goals are compatible with the position on offer.

If applicants won't be able to use the available position to advance or fulfil their career goals, you're taking a risk by hiring them. Such applicants may be easily enticed to leave your organization for greener pastures – opportunities that are more in line with their career goals.

Achievements

To get the best candidates for the job, you should assess applicants' past achievements and results. These can point you to the applicants most likely to become high-performing employees in your company.

For example, an applicant worth considering may have consistently achieved promotions, contributed to significant financial savings or profits, or acted as a leader who assisted junior employees in another company.

An online magazine has posted an advertisement for a new content editor. Casey, the Human Resources manager, receives numerous resumes for the position. He now needs to screen those resumes.

First, Casey reviews the job description for the position and chooses an important job requirement to use for the initial scan of the resumes.

The Overview of the content editor job description is: "edits and prepares content for publication on site, liaises with content providers and uploads edited submissions, writes content and provides marketing material when necessary, and maintains records of submissions and publications."

Reporting structure: this position is part of the Editing Department and reports to the editor. They will also liaise with journalists and freelancers regarding preparation of content.

Tasks and responsibilities: prepares content for publication on site; communicates standards and edits to content producers; uploads edited submissions to site; administers team leave and overtime records; writes and updates marketing content for site; and keeps records of submissions and publications.

Qualifications and skills: undergraduate degree in journalism, communications, or a related field; three to five years editing experience in an online environment; in-depth knowledge of web-based content management systems; excellent proofreading skills; good interpersonal communication skills; good time management skills; and good attention to detail.

One prerequisite is that the editor who's hired must be able to write effective marketing content.

Casey uses this attribute as his criterion for discarding several resumes from unsuitable applicants. This leaves him with a much smaller pile of resumes to consider.

Casey then moves on to detailed screening of ten remaining candidates, one of whom is Myra Cabricci. He looks closely at her resume, identifying her specific knowledge, experience, qualifications, and career goals.

Question

Which of the job requirements does Myra's resume line up with?

Myra's Objective section reads: "To build experience in traditional and new media publications, and eventually start my own media company."

Myra's "Attributes, skills, and achievements" section reads: "Strong communication skills. Excellent editing skills. Ability to multi-task and work quickly. Very basic knowledge of intranet / Internet-based content management systems. Wrote some of Chitown Monthly's most successful marketing material to date, and developed a comprehensive system to track article submissions and publication."

Myra's "Career highlights" section states that from June 2007 to the present day, she is the online editor at the Chicago-based "Chitown Monthly." Prior to that, from October 2003 to July 2006, she was a junior reporter at the same publication. Before that, from July 2001 to May 2003, she was a corporate communications intern at BlazerFire Media Inc, based in Boston.

Myra's Education section states that she attended Chicago's Southbranch University from September 1996 to May 2001. She obtained a Bachelor of Arts in Communications, with Honors.

Options:
1. Qualifications
2. Specific knowledge

3. Career goals
4. Experience

Answer:

Option 1: This is a correct option. Myra holds an honors-level degree in communications, giving her the educational qualifications needed for the position.

Option 2: This option is incorrect. The position calls for in-depth knowledge of content management systems, but Myra only has very basic knowledge of this subject.

Option 3: This is a correct option. The advertised position is in line with Myra's immediate career goals. And it will also help her to progress toward her long-term professional ambitions in the media industry.

Option 4: This option is correct. Myra's online editing experience falls within the years cited in the job description. In addition, she has also worked in corporate communications and journalism.

Based on his detailed screening, Casey identifies Myra as a potential candidate who meets all the expectations for the job, other than specific knowledge. But, because she generally seems like a good fit for the position, he adds her to the shortlist of candidates he'll contact to invite to interviews.

Rating resumes

As you do detailed screening on a resume, try to keep other resumes in mind. You need to consider the resumes in relation to one another.

For example, while going through a pile of resumes, you may notice a group of four candidates who excel in terms of relevant work experience and qualifications.

As you screen each resume, keep this group in mind, setting them as an important standard by which you measure candidates in the rest of the pile.

You may use a rating system to help you assess how well resumes match up to the job requirements, as well as how they rate in relation to one another.

Rating – or ranking – each resume on a scale can help you sort a pile of resumes, quickly prioritizing ones that have the best scores.

So once you have checked how well each resume meets the requirements spelled out in the job description, you can rate or mark resumes to indicate those with excellent attributes that surpass the requirements and, finally, divide the resumes into categories.

See each step to find out about one method of rating resumes.

1. Rate resumes

Check whether an applicant appears to be superior or impressive in terms of relevant work experience, on-the-job achievements, training and qualifications, and visual or linguistic presentation of the resume.

If the applicant excels in any area, put a dot in the corner of the resume. You might use two dots if the candidate is extremely impressive in a particular area.

2. Divide into categories

Set up three work spaces, marked "outstanding applicants," "average applicants," and "backup applicants." Now sort through the pile of resumes, putting the resumes with the most dots in the "outstanding applicants" category; resumes with the next highest number of dots in the "average applicants" category; and resumes with few or no dots in the "backup applicants" category.

At the end of this step, you'll have divided the applicants into three groups and you can more easily decide which applicants you want to call in for interviews.

Bear in mind that the suggested process for rating resumes is only a guideline. You can adapt or alter it based on your particular situation to develop a rating system that will be effective and easy for you to use.

Case Study: Question 1 of 3
Scenario

You need to hire a librarian to work at the company's head office, and have received numerous responses to the job advertisement you placed. You're now in the process of screening three applicants' resumes.

Answer the questions in the given order to screen the resumes so that you can select the best applicant of the three.

Question

Using education as a deciding factor, which candidates would you screen out during a quick overview?

Options:

1. Faye Oprisan
2. Ralph McCall
3. Natasha Sands

Answer:

Option 1: This is an incorrect option. Even though Faye doesn't have a postgraduate degree in LIS, she does have an undergraduate degree in it.

Option 2: This option is incorrect. Ralph holds both honors' and masters' qualifications in Library and

Information Science. This qualification is listed on the job description.

Option 3: This is a correct option. Natasha doesn't have the required postgraduate qualification in Library and Information Science, so she should be screened out at this point.

Case Study: Question 2 of 3

You've applied crosses to candidates' resumes, based on their level of superiority or achievement in specific categories. One cross indicates an average level, two crosses is for good, and three crosses is for excellent. You then put the highest-scoring resumes into a "Pile A," while good and average resumes go to "Pile B" and "Pile C" respectively.

Which candidate would you put into "Pile A" and definitely consider further?

Options:

1. Faye Oprisan
2. Ralph McCall

Answer:

Option 1: This option is incorrect. In the rating system, Faye doesn't get quite as many crosses as Ralph. She has a high score for knowledge, but scores poorly in the other areas under consideration.

Option 2: This is the correct option. In the rating system, Ralph scores more crosses than Faye. He scores excellently in knowledge, qualifications, and career objectives. He also scores relatively well in experience.

Case Study: Question 3 of 3

Why is the resume for Faye Oprisan not as strong as that for Ralph McCall?

Options:

1. Faye's knowledge of financial services seems inferior to Ralph's
2. Faye is less academically qualified than Ralph is
3. Faye's career objective doesn't relate to the advertised job
4. Faye doesn't have as much relevant work experience as Ralph

Answer:

Option 1: This is an incorrect option. Both candidates have a high level of financial services knowledge – which the job description calls for. Both have also studied in the field after obtaining their university degrees.

Option 2: This is a correct option. The job description calls for a postgraduate qualification in Library and Information Science. In terms of education, Ralph holds honors' and masters' degrees in the relevant subject, whereas Faye holds a bachelor's degree. However, this may not matter in the end, if experience and other skills outweigh the academic qualifications.

Option 3: This option is incorrect. The advertised job of corporate librarian does support Faye's career objective – it can give her the experience she desires.

Option 4: This is a correct option. The job description calls for at least three years experience in an information management position, preferably in a financial services environment. Ralph is considerably more experienced than Faye, particularly in the corporate context. Faye is still starting out in her career, and hasn't worked in a financial-based library for a significant amount of time.

Benefits of screening resumes

When you need to hire someone, it's important to establish a resume screening process.

Question

What do you think are the benefits of being able to screen resumes effectively?

Options:

1. You'll make better-informed hiring decisions
2. You'll be able to determine whether the advertised position is actually necessary
3. You'll have more time for interviews
4. You'll hire the right person for the job every time

Answer:

Option 1: This is a correct option. By using resume screening, you'll know what to look for in an applicant, which will give you more confidence in your ability to weed out unsuitable applicants.

Option 2: This option is incorrect. Determining the necessity of the job occurs in the process of developing a job description, which comes well before resume screening.

Option 3: This option is correct. Resume screening effectively weeds out inappropriate applicants, so you can spend less time considering unsuitable applicants and more time interviewing promising ones.

Option 4: This is an incorrect option. Although resume screening helps you to make better-informed hiring decisions, it doesn't guarantee that you'll choose the best possible applicant for every vacancy.

Screening resumes helps you to match appropriate applicants to the job you're advertising.

Screening can be a huge time-saver and can enhance your ability to hire the best candidates for each position you advertise.

Screening resumes can be a time-consuming process. Fortunately, you can automate parts of this process using electronic screening software.

The electronic screening process for a resume consists of four steps:
1. scan the resume into the system, using optical character-recognition software,
2. check the resulting document and correct any errors that may have occurred,
3. classify the document's information into pre-defined categories, such as the applicant's qualifications and skills, and
4. store the document in a database, which you can search when seeking candidates for a particular position.

Electronic screening has several advantages over manual screening. These include saved time, objectivity, a reduction in paperwork, and easier communication with job candidates.

See each area to find out how electronic screening enhances it.

Time

Using electronic screening reduces the time it takes for recruiters to search for potential candidates, freeing up time for them to perform other tasks.

Objectivity

Electronic screening helps eliminate human bias in the screening process. Software simply searches for specific information, consistently applying the same, objective criteria.

Paperwork

Electronic screening makes it unnecessary for recruiters to physically file and manage paper resumes.

Communication

Electronic screening software can speed up communication with candidates, enabling you to send automatic response letters to candidates once their resumes are received.

Resume screening is an important activity that can save you time and help you make better-informed hiring decisions. Screening involves sifting through resumes and assessing them against predetermined job requirements to identify the applicants it makes sense to interview for a position.

The basic process for screening resumes includes a quick overview – which speedily eliminates many unsuitable applicants – and then more detailed screening of the remaining resumes.

During detailed screening, you can use a rating system to simplify the process of sorting applicants' resumes. This can help you identify those applicants it's best to proceed with interviewing.

RED FLAGS

Red flags

Recognizing red flags

In addition to checking resumes to determine if applicants meet job requirements, you need to assess each resume on its own merits. This type of screening can be unpredictable, because each resume may be unique in its style.

As you screen resumes, you should also look for "red flags" – warning signals that something is not quite right about the applicant or this person's apparent suitability for a position.

Question

Which do you think are some typical examples of red flags in resumes?

Options:

1. Overemphasis on hobbies or non-work interests
2. Vague statements about responsibilities
3. Lack of academic qualifications from prestigious institutions

4. Job hopping
5. Lack of promotion within a company
6. Sloppy resume appearance
7. Failure to work for a range of different companies
8. Unexplained career gaps

Answer:

Common red flags are unexplained career gaps, job hopping, vague statements about responsibilities, lack of promotion within a company, sloppy resume appearance, and overemphasis on hobbies or non-work interests.

Unexplained career gaps are periods when a resume doesn't indicate that the applicant was either working or studying. For example, a resume may specify that an applicant left one job in May 2007 but started in a new position only early in April 2010.

These gaps commonly indicate periods when the applicant was unemployed.

But it could be that the candidate is concealing information.

For example, an applicant may not be proud of a career gap spent in any of these ways:

- in a rehabilitation center treating a substance abuse problem,
- suffering from depression, unable to search for a job, or
- Incarcerated.

In your experience, you may have found that a candidate had a good reason for a career gap. For example, the candidate might have taken time off for any of these reasons:

- to serve in the military,
- to travel,

- to take care of a sick parent, child, or other family member,
- to recover from a serious injury or illness, or
- to be with a new child.

Job hopping refers to a pattern in which a candidate repeatedly works in one job only for a relatively short period, and then moves on to another job.

Job hopping could signal instability or a recurring problem that the candidate has not successfully dealt with.

For example, a candidate who has worked seven different jobs in the last 18 months may have a problem with authority – leading to repeated resignations or dismissals.

However, job hopping might also indicate that candidates haven't yet found a job that meets their requirements – in which case, you'd have to think closely about whether your vacancy really suits their needs.

Or job hopping could be strategic. Some candidates may identify job hopping as a way to build a professional network, to keep progressing in their career, and to maintain passion by consistently taking on new challenges.

Whatever the case, if you identify a candidate as being a job hopper, you need to find out why this pattern keeps occurring. You need to confirm whether the candidate is likely to stay in the advertised job for the period of time you require.

Vague statements about responsibilities fail to explain exactly what the candidate's tasks were in one or more previous jobs. This type of red flag could indicate a lack of definition or an inflated job title.

See each possible reason for vagueness in a resume for more information about it.

Lack of definition

A previous employer might have failed to define the candidate's job clearly. The result could be that, despite knowing exactly what the job entailed, the candidate repeats the vague wording used in the employer's job description in a resume.

Inflated job title

Candidates might use misleading job titles to exaggerate their levels of authority or responsibility in previous jobs. If the title doesn't seem to match the responsibilities listed, you may want to find out why.

The descriptions should indicate the relationship of the job to what the company does to stay in business.

Also keep an eye out for ambiguous phrases, such as "participated in," "assisted with," and "in association with."

This kind of wording may convey the idea that the candidate has solid experience in an area – but in reality, the candidate may have done very little of the relevant work.

Similarly, the phrase "familiar with" could indicate anything from strong knowledge on a subject to very minimal knowledge.

While reviewing a resume, you may find that a candidate changes jobs but keeps moving into new jobs at the same level – for example, into middle management positions.

Or you may find that the candidate has held the same position at a single company for an unusually long time.

A lack of promotion within a company or across a career suggests that the candidate is not advancing to greater levels of responsibility and more important work.

This could indicate that the candidate doesn't do a good job. Or perhaps the candidate likes staying in a comfort zone and lacks the ambition to push for a promotion.

However, this red flag might also be inevitable, given the candidate's circumstances.

For example, the candidate may hold a very specialized job, such as a pilot or antiques appraiser.

Or it may be impossible for the candidate to attain a higher position until the senior person in that role either retires or resigns.

A resume may be sloppy in appearance because it's untidy or contains spelling or grammatical mistakes, typographical errors, poor punctuation, or other forms of errors such as inconsistent capitalization.

Resumes with many of these mistakes can indicate that the candidate has inadequate presentation skills. Or the candidate isn't serious enough about the position to put in the time and effort to create a resume that's presentable.

When a candidate's resume places overemphasis on hobbies or non-work interests, hiring the candidate may expose you to a number of risks – including potentially irresponsible behavior and lack of commitment to the advertised position.

See each risk to find out more about it.

Potentially irresponsible behavior

Although candidates may enjoy dangerous and risky activities in their free time, you should be very careful if these activities could seriously impact the candidate's work-related performance.

Hobbies can tell you a bit about someone's personality, so if you are hiring for a desk job, and someone emphasizes active hobbies and extensive travel, it may throw up a red flag. That's not to say that people with active hobbies can't work at a desk, but it's something to think about.

Lack of commitment

A candidate may overemphasize activities or events unrelated to the advertised position due to a lack of real interest in that position. In this case, the position probably doesn't align with the candidate's honest career aspirations.

This could result in the candidate being reluctant to work extra hours or abandoning your company as soon as a "better" job opportunity arises.

Dealing with red flags

Sometimes you come across a resume that, at first, seems to identify a perfect candidate who meets all the job requirements.

On closer inspection, though, you spot a red flag issue.

If you feel the candidate is right for an interview in this case, you should highlight the issue and make a note to address it during the interview.

While going through a resume, you can make notes or marks to highlight red flag issues that you want to follow up on. For example, you may employ a system that uses the letters "C," "D," and "T."

See each letter to find out how to use it in highlighting red flag issues.

C

C stands for clarify. If you find vague statements, or you're confused about an item on a resume, you place a

"C" on that item to remind you to get clarification on the issue when you interview the candidate.

For example, the phrase "Eight people reported to me" doesn't say much about a person's responsibilities. Who were these people? Why did they report to the candidate? Did the candidate simply delegate tasks to them? Did the candidate also conduct their performance reviews?

D

D stands for define. When you come across a term that you don't understand, place a "D" on the term to remind you to ask the candidate to define the term in the interview. Typically, you'll place a "D" on unfamiliar technical or industry-specific terms. For example, you may have no idea that the term "malvertising" is just a blended version of the phrase "malicious online advertising."

You can also use a "D" for terms or phrases that are not clearly defined. For example, "hardware orientation program" doesn't really explain what the relevant program entailed.

T

T stands for tighten. When a certain detail in a resume is not specific enough, place a "T" on that detail to remind you that you need to ask the candidate for substantiating information. Information that may need tightening could include dates, growth statistics, and multiple positions in the same company.

For example, a candidate may list a certain job as running from "2003 to 2004." This period could encompass anything from two months to two full years. Similarly, a sales increase specified as 50% may not be so impressive if the original sales figure was very low.

The "CDT" method is one, relatively simple way of dealing with red flag issues.

Other methods exist, and you can even come up with your own system via trial and error.

But if you've decided that some candidates are unsuitable – based on their resumes – make sure you're excluding them for the right reasons. You should always avoid letting your unconscious biases influence your decisions about which candidates to interview. Two areas of unconscious bias are personal preferences and potentially discriminatory information.

See each area of unconscious bias to find out more about it.

Personal preferences

Although you may think your decisions are based on professional criteria alone, sometimes your personal preferences may play a role in your thinking.

For example, you may automatically favor a candidate who graduated from your alma mater, or you may subconsciously dismiss candidates who list hobbies you find uninteresting.

Potentially discriminatory information

When candidates include information such as their age, race, religion, or number of dependents, it becomes possible that you'll discriminate against them based on these attributes.

For example, you may automatically decide against a candidate you know is older than most other staff in your company. Or you may feel sympathy for the financial burden of a candidate with four children and favor this person over others unfairly.

It's vital to prevent this type of discrimination from affecting your decisions.

To ensure you remain objective, remember to focus on each candidate's ability to do the job. Try to block out factors that don't directly relate to the candidate's likely on-the-job performance.

Case Study: Question 1 of 3

Scenario

You're reviewing resumes for an assistant corporate librarian position. You want to check three particular resumes for any red flag issues.

Answer the questions in any order.

Question

Which red flags can you find in Vincent Simpson's resume?

Options:

1. Unclear statements about knowledge and work achievements
2. Spelling errors in the "Objective" section
3. Lack of promotion to higher positions
4. An unexplained career gap at the end of 2009

Answer:

Option 1: This option is correct. Vincent used ambiguous statements to describe his knowledge of financial services legislation and his contribution to the university's audit.

Option 2: This is an incorrect option. Vincent's resume doesn't contain any spelling mistakes.

Option 3: This is a correct option. Vincent's first job was as a junior librarian for 18 months. However, his next job was also as a junior librarian – even though by the time he started it, he had completed a postgraduate diploma.

Option 4: This option is incorrect. Vincent took a two-month course from December 2009 to January 2010.

Case Study: Question 2 of 3

Identify the red flags in Imogene Vega's resume.

Options:

1. Inability to keep a job for a long period
2. Overemphasis of interest in journalism
3. An unexplained career gap between 2004 and 2006
4. Vague information about her role on a library catalog digitization project

Answer:

Option 1: This is an incorrect option. All of Imogene's jobs have been relatively stable. Her shortest period of employment was 19 months, and that was her first job out of college, so it's not too unusual.

Option 2: This option is correct. Imogene puts special emphasis on the success she's had in journalism – an endeavor that seems, from the way she has written her resume, to consume a lot of her time.

Option 3: This is a correct option. Imogene's job at Keane Secondary School ended in August 2004. Her next job began in May 2006. No work or studies are listed in her resume for the 20 months in between.

Option 4: This option is incorrect. Imogene's resume clearly notes her roles as project manager and chief tester on the digitization project.

Case Study: Question 3 of 3

Which red flags are in Kimberly Miles's resume?

Options:

1. Short periods of time at each job

2. Overemphasis on an interest in information management
3. Lack of career progression between jobs
4. Numerous spelling and grammatical mistakes

Answer:

Option 1: This option is correct. Because Kimberly's jobs have only lasted for a few months at a time, she appears to be job hopping.

Option 2: This is an incorrect option. Kimberly's expressed interest in information management is relevant to the assistant corporate librarian job she's applying for.

Option 3: This option is incorrect. Kimberly's work history shows definite career progression. She has moved from the position of secretary, to office administrator, to office manager.

Option 4: This is a correct option. All four sections of Kimberly's resume contain mistakes, giving the resume a sloppy appearance.

Sometimes a resume may contain warning signs – or red flags – that can alert you to potential risks in hiring a job candidate. Common red flags include unexplained career gaps, job hopping, vague statements about responsibilities, lack of promotion, sloppy resume appearance, and overemphasis on hobbies or non-work interests.

You should highlight all red flag issues for candidates you don't choose to exclude from further consideration so that you can follow up on them with the candidate. However, if you decide to exclude candidates based on their resumes, ensure that no personal bias has influenced your decisions.

CHAPTER II - PREPARING TO INTERVIEW

CHAPTER II - Preparing to Interview

In this chapter, you'll learn the following essentials for preparing to interview:
- how best to prepare before conducting an interview,
- the five common errors interviewers make, so that you can avoid these when you're preparing for and conducting interviews, and
- the relevant legal issues, so you know what it is and isn't appropriate to include in interviews.

PREPARE TO INTERVIEW

Prepare to interview

Preparing for interviews

The success of an interview depends on steps you perform at the start of the recruitment process – for example, you perform a job analysis, create a job description, and carefully review resumes against the job requirements detailed in the job description. These steps help you narrow down the list of candidates you'll invite to interview. And once you've done this, it's time to determine how you will conduct the actual interviews.

The process of preparing effectively for an interview includes four steps:
- determine the structure of the interview,
- review the necessary paperwork and plan questions,
- schedule enough time for the interview, and
- plan an appropriate environment in which to conduct the interview.

Determine structure

Prior to asking candidates to come in for interviews, you need to decide how the interviews will be structured.

To determine this, try answering five questions:
- How many rounds of interviews are required?
- How many interviews should be allocated per round?
- Who should conduct the interviews?
- How many interviewers should be allocated to each interview?
- How much time is required for each interview?

See each question for more information about planning the structure of the interviews.

How many rounds?

Think about the number of times candidates will have to come to your company to complete the interview process. Will they have to come in only once, or will you, for example, ask a set of candidates to come in a second time for additional questions or to meet with another interviewer? Each separate visit to your company is considered one round.

How many interviews per round?

It's important to determine how many interviews per round are necessary. Sometimes it's only necessary for candidates to go through one interview per round, but there may be occasions when several are required.

For instance, two managers from different departments may want to interview candidates in two separate interviews.

Who should conduct the interviews?

Give some thought to who in your organization should meet with candidates. For example, are any supervisors or managers trained specifically to conduct interviews? Also, who knows most about what's required of the successful job applicant and should participate in identifying the best candidate? These are the individuals you should consider asking to conduct interviews.

How many interviewers?

Just one interviewer or a panel of interviewers may need to conduct the interviews. The best approach will depend on the situation.

For instance, if you have several rounds of interviews, it may be suitable to have one-to-one interviews. If you have fewer rounds but many managers who need to meet each candidate, you may want a panel interview at some point.

How much time?

Think carefully about how much time you should devote to different requirements and to different parts of each interview. This will help you structure the content of the interviews. It also ensures both interviewers and candidates can be given realistic expectations about how long the interviews will take to complete.

Generally, an interview can be divided into three phases – the opening, body, and closing. When you're determining how much time is required for each interview, it's important to account for each of these phases.

See each phase for details of what it involves and what percentage of the available time you should allocate to it.

Opening

During the opening phase, you meet a candidate, put this person at ease, and explain the structure of the interview. You should allocate about 10% of the total time for the interview to this phase.

Body

During the body phase, you evaluate the candidates' suitability for the job by reviewing their qualifications, skills, understanding, and experience. This should take up about 80% of the allocated time.

Closing

During the closing phase, you use the remaining 10% of the time to thank the candidate for coming in, ask for any questions or comments, and explain how the follow-up procedure will work.

Rachel works as an HR consultant for a modeling agency and has to set up interviews to hire a receptionist for the company's new offices. Follow along as Rachel reviews the five questions she should consider when determining the structure of the interviews.

Rachel first thinks about how many rounds the interview should be comprised of. She decides that there will be two rounds – the first to interview all candidates and the second to interview the two candidates identified as the most suitable.

She then considers how many interviews should be carried out per round. She decides only one interview per round will be required. Rachel will be conducting the first eight interviews with the office manager. The office manager will conduct the second round of interviews.

Two interviewers will be present during the first round and just one for the second round. Rachel assesses the time it'll take her to gain enough information about the candidates and give them an overview of the company and the position. She estimates she needs 30 minutes.

Question

Bob has a list of candidates to interview for a copy editing job at the newspaper.

Which are effective ways to determine the structure for the interview?

Options:

1. Calculate how long to spend on questions about the candidate's copy editing experience

2. Decide if he needs to bring each candidate in on two or more different days

3. Ask the managing editor who will work with the new copy editor to help interview the candidates

4. Determine whether a panel interview is suitable for the first round of interviews

5. Set aside time to rewrite the job description based on the experience of the candidates to interview

6. Set a time for the interview and contact the candidates to determine whether the time suits them

Answer:

Option 1: This is a correct option. Bob needs to think about how much time he has to set aside for specific questions he has to ask during the interview. He can then allocate this time to essential elements of the interview, such as time to discuss each candidate's experience.

Option 2: This option is correct. Bob has to think about how many rounds of interviews are required. This will determine the number of times candidates will have to come to the company to complete the interview process.

Option 3: This option is correct. To structure the interview effectively, Bob has to know who will meet with and interview the candidates, and whether or not these individuals are adequately trained in, or have enough experience with, interviewing.

Option 4: This is a correct option. To plan an effective interview structure, it's important for Bob to know how many interviewers will be necessary according to the specifics of the situation and the job being applied for.

Option 5: This option is incorrect. The job description should not be rewritten, as it determines which candidates are most suitable and is a useful tool during the interview process for narrowing down the list of candidates that should be considered for the position.

Option 6: This is an incorrect option. The time of an interview should not be centered around what's most suitable for the candidate, but rather how much time will be necessary to carry out all the aspects of the interview.

Review paperwork and plan questions

Before conducting interviews, you need to review all the relevant paperwork.

You first read through the job description so you're clear on what skills, experience, personal attributes, training, and qualifications you need to search for in candidates.

You can then review each candidate's resume and any other relevant documents – for example, completed application forms or certificates from educational institutions.

After reviewing all necessary paperwork, use the information you've obtained to develop questions to ask each candidate.

You should plan a series of questions that cover key requirements for the available position, ensuring that all the questions are directly job-related.

To develop a good line of questioning, you formulate questions based on statements in candidates' resumes that relate to key job requirements. For example, a key requirement for a librarian position is "to establish and implement library and information policies." A candidate's resume states that the person "implemented essential information policies" for a law library. A question you derive from this is "What were the policies and how did you implement them?"

Deriving questions from statements

Questions that you could develop from this statement include "What aspects of their work did you supervise?" or "How many staff members did you supervise?" Your questions should always relate to the key job requirements.

Although it helps to prepare some basic questions to ask during interviews, don't develop too many questions or be too specific at this point.

If you are, you may end up simply reading from a long, detailed list of questions, and sounding stiff and formal. This won't put the candidate at ease.

You're may also end up asking questions the candidate has already answered in response to others on your list. The candidate may wonder whether you are listening.

Try to prepare some broad-based questions.

As the interview progresses, other questions that need to be asked will follow naturally from the interviewee's answers.

Using an interview preparation form can help you organize yourself for the interview. You can include on it all the information you have gathered from the relevant paperwork, as well as the basic questions you want to ask. It can help you stay focused during the interview.

Question

Bob needs to review the paperwork and prepare some questions for interviews for a copy editing position.

Which are effective ways to do this?

Options:

1. Use the information from the job description and the candidate's resume to develop some basic questions for the interview

2. Organize the information he's gathered about the candidate and the job and put it on a form that he can bring into the interview

3. Do a job analysis to determine that the appropriate requirements have been included in the job description

4. Prepare detailed questions for all the key aspects of the job so he has a script to follow for the interview

Answer:

Option 1: This is a correct option. Developing some broad-based questions related to job requirements and the applicant's resume will help prepare you for the interview. You need to review the job description and each resume to develop these questions.

Option 2: This option is correct. Some interviewers use an interview preparation form as a handy way of organizing information for each interview.

Option 3: This option is incorrect. Conducting a job analysis is done before preparing for the actual interview. It supplies the information for the job description, which you'll use to prepare for the interview.

Option 4: This is an incorrect option. Keeping to a script will make an interview stiff and formal, and may make the candidate uneasy. It can also mean you ask questions that the candidate has already answered when responding to another question.

Schedule enough time

You've determined the interview structure, reviewed relevant paperwork, and formulated appropriate questions. Now you can schedule a suitable amount of time for the interview.

Scheduling enough time for the interview means allocating time for pre-interview preparation, which includes reviewing the paperwork and planning questions, and time for the actual face-to-face interview.

It also means taking into account post-interview activities, such as compiling notes, assessing interviews, contacting candidate references, and making additional appointments.

The time you need to allocate to the face-to-face phase of the process will vary, depending on the purpose and scope of the interview. Typically, an employment interview will take from 30 minutes up to 60 minutes.

And the pre- and post-interview stages will typically require from 5 to 15 minutes each. Giving yourself time after an interview enables you to make notes about previous candidates, familiarize yourself with the next candidate, and take a breather – which is particularly helpful when you're meeting with several candidates throughout the day.

Some interviewers like to avoid planning interviews for the middle of the day. It's often best to hold interviews early in the day.

This is because you're more energized and focused at the start of the day and you'll have fewer distractions or interruptions.

If you cannot plan interviews for the early morning, ensure you give yourself enough time, prior to meeting with your first candidate, to clear your mind and switch your focus from what you've been doing during the day.

Once you've been able to schedule adequate time for your interviews, you can invite the candidates to come in to meet with you.

As far as possible, when inviting candidates to an interview, try to give them sufficient notice of their meeting with you.

You can call the candidate to agree on a mutually convenient time and then follow this up with a formal e-mail or letter of confirmation.

The formal e-mail or letter of confirmation should include these types of details:
- the agreed time and date of the interview,
- how long the interview will likely last,
- the location where the interview will take place – you may need to provide a map,
- any documents and samples the candidate should bring, and
- the names of interviewers.

The documents or samples that an interviewee may be asked to bring to the interview vary.

For example, you might need relevant certificates confirming the individual's qualifications, a valid driver's license, or examples of work, such as writing samples or artwork.

While preparing for her interviews, Rachel allocates specific time to all the tasks she needs to perform. She decides that for the first round of interviews, she'll interview two candidates per day over four days. For the second round, she'll need only one day. She calls each candidate and arranges a mutually convenient time in the morning, and then sends out a formal letter of confirmation detailing time and date, duration, location, and required documentation.

Question

Bob needs to schedule time for his interviews with candidates for a copy editing position.

Which are effective ways to do this?

Options:

1. Allow 45 minutes for the interview, as well as 15 minutes for preparation and 5 minutes for after the interview

2. Schedule the interviews for a time when he has the most energy and focus

3. Give candidates no more than two days' notice when calling to invite them for an interview

4. Schedule interviews back-to-back so he can fit as many as possible in the morning

Answer:

Option 1: This option is correct. Scheduling enough time for the interview includes allocating time for pre-interview preparation and post-interview activities, as well as for the face-to-face meeting.

Option 2: This is a correct option. It can help to plan interviews for early in the day. This is because you tend to have more energy and focus at the start of the day.

Option 3: This option is incorrect. You need to give candidates sufficient notice for an interview. Two days may not be enough time for candidates to fit interviews into their schedules.

Option 4: This is an incorrect option. You often need a breather in between interviews to allow you to organize your notes on the candidate and refocus on the next candidate.

Plan the environment

The final step in preparing for interviews is to plan where best to conduct the interviews. The three important factors to consider here are privacy, freedom from distractions, and comfort.

See each factor to find out more about it.

Privacy

It's important to ensure that the environment in which you interview candidates is private. During interviews, you'll be asking candidates questions about their work experiences. It's inappropriate for you to ask these questions in front of others, with whom they could be working if they got the job. You want the candidates to feel comfortable and be forthcoming with information.

Freedom from distractions

You should choose a location in which you and the candidates you'll be interviewing will be relatively free from distractions. These include ringing phones, e-mail or instant message alerts, general office noise, and interruptions from colleagues.

Guard too against becoming mentally distracted during interviews – remind yourself to stay focused.

Comfort

It's important to choose a location in which both you and the interviewee will be comfortable. This will help you both relax, focus, and ensure that the interview is productive.

Factors like the type and arrangement of furniture in a room, as well as room temperature, can affect comfort levels.

Rachel's office has an open-plan design and is often noisy, with ringing telephones and conversations taking place between office colleagues.

So Rachel decides to use a small boardroom as her interview room. This means she and the candidates she interviews won't be disrupted, and can speak privately and comfortably.

Question

Bob needs to decide where to hold the interviews for a copy editing position.

Which are effective ways to plan for the interview environment?

Options:

1. Seek a place that's free from noise and potential interruptions

2. Set up a chair next to his desk so the candidates get a sense of the atmosphere in the office

3. Make sure the furniture in the interviewing room is not too formally arranged

4. Ensure you have a phone in the room so you can take important calls related to your regular duties

Answer:

Option 1: This is a correct option. The interview is a private meeting in which you and the candidate focus on the requirements of the open position. Distractions may mean you don't get as full a picture of the candidate's background and you won't be able to make a proper assessment.

Option 2: This option is incorrect. When you interview candidates, you need to have privacy. You can explain the atmosphere in the office to the candidate if it's relevant or if the candidate is curious about it.

Option 3: This option is correct. Making sure you and the candidates are comfortable will put everyone more at ease during the interview.

Option 4: This option is incorrect. When you schedule interviews, you need clear time away from your regular duties to focus on the finding the right person. You don't want distractions during the interview.

Thorough preparation is a crucial element in the success of job interviews.

To prepare effectively for interviews, you should determine how best to structure the interviews, review necessary paperwork and plan interview questions, schedule enough time for each interview, and identify an appropriate environment in which to hold the interviews.

COMMON INTERVIEWING ERRORS

Common interviewing errors

Being aware of common errors

As an interviewer, it's easy to fall into bad habits. Being aware of some of the common errors interviewers make can help ensure you don't fall into the same traps during your interviews.

Take Graham, for example. Graham interviews Myra for the position of research analyst. A job requirement for this position is the ability to interpret and analyze data.

He didn't have much time to prepare before the interview. When he asks Myra if she has experience in research, he nods when she says "Yes – two years." He then asks her about her experiences as a radiologist, an area he's particularly interested in.

Graham is impressed by Myra's knowledge of radiology and uses most of the remaining time of the interview to chat to her about it.

Graham assumes that because Myra has a radiology qualification, she can do research.

He then goes on to tell her about his company, providing as much detail as he can – including information like what employee benefits the company provides.

Before he knows it, he has spent 15 minutes talking about the company and the allotted time for the interview is up.

Question

How would you rate Graham as an interviewer, based on his interview with Myra?

Options:

1. Excellent
2. Average
3. Poor

Answer:

Option 1: Graham may be an excellent interviewer, but he doesn't display it in his interview with Myra. He isn't prepared, asks ineffective questions, and talks too much. These are three of the most common errors that interviewers make.

Option 2: In his interview with Myra, Graham gives a below average performance as he shows a lack of preparation, focuses on irrelevant work experience, and makes assumptions.

Option 3: Graham doesn't conduct his interview effectively. He shows he's unprepared and focuses on an area of Myra's experience that isn't relevant to the key job requirement. Graham also makes an assumption and spends too much time talking instead of asking effective questions.

Graham doesn't get the information he needs to determine Myra's suitability for the research position. He makes several common interviewing errors – lack of preparation, asking ineffective questions, talking too much, and not listening. Other common errors are not controlling an interview – with the result that it goes off course – and failing to challenge assumptions.

Lack of preparation

Not preparing properly is one of the most common mistakes. No interview is likely to be a success if you haven't read the candidate's resume, you're unfamiliar with the job requirements, and you don't know what questions to ask. If this is the case, you won't get the information you need to make a real assessment of the candidate's suitability for the job.

Follow along as Dean interviews Jeffrey for a position as marketing team lead.

Dean: I've read your resume and understand you have marketing experience. Jeffrey: Yes, I worked with a firm for three years and was promoted to head

Dean: OK. So, what did you do before that?

Jeffrey: I did an internship for six months and then the company decided to employ me as a marketing assistant. It's all there on my resume.

Dean: OK. Um, that sounds good. Tell me about your education.

Jeffrey: I completed a masters degree in marketing and business management

Dean: Great. That's good. Is there anything that's not on your resume that you'd like to tell me about?

Jeffrey: Well, I'm not exactly sure what you'd like to focus on?

Dean: No other learning experiences, for instance?

Jeffrey: I've had lots of those, but I'm just not sure what you'd be most interested in hearing about.

Question

Which is the main problem with Dean's questions in the interview?

Options:

1. They're too general
2. They're not relevant for the position
3. They focus too much on education

Answer:

The main problem here is that Dean's questions are too general and don't elicit enough from the candidate. They're relevant in that they focus on experience and education related to the job, but they don't get into the specifics, jumping from one bit of information on the resume to the next.

From the interview, it's clear Dean didn't prepare adequately beforehand.

He asks only very general questions, instead of focusing on finding out whether Jeffrey could meet the specific requirements associated with the available position.

He also wastes time because he focuses on information already available in Jeffrey's resume. He fails to delve any deeper by asking more specific questions.

Two main strategies can ensure that, unlike Dean, you're properly prepared for an interview:

- define your requirements – based on the requirements outlined in the relevant job description – so you know exactly what you're looking for and can ask relevant questions, and

- plan an interview strategy beforehand so you know how to proceed with getting the information you require from the candidate.

Asking ineffective questions

Another common interviewing error is asking ineffective questions – ones that don't elicit the information you require. These questions can waste time. And if too many of your questions fall in this category, the interview probably won't reveal whether the candidate is really suitable for the job.

Ineffective questions often result from these types of errors on the part of the interviewer:

unintentionally diverging from focus on finding out whether the candidate fulfills the job requirements

asking close-ended instead of open-ended questions, and failing to ask the "why" behind the "what"

See each cause of ineffective questions for more information about it.

Diverging from focus

If you don't have a plan and don't use a job description, it's very easy to diverge from what's relevant during an interview.

For example, if someone is being interviewed for the position of recruitment consultant – where the main requirement is sales experience – and the interviewer starts focusing on the candidate's background in IT, the interviewer is diverging from the focus of the interview.

Asking closed-ended questions

Interviewers often make the mistake of asking close-ended questions, which prompt a candidate to respond with just a "yes" or "no." These questions often begin with words like "did you," "have you," or "are you." Most candidates will elaborate but some candidates, who take more urging to get talking, may not respond well to these types of questions.

An example of a close-ended question is "Do you have sales experience?" A much better, open-ended question to ask would be "What kind of sales experience do you have and what have you learned from it?"

Failing to ask "why"

Interviewers who ask "what" questions and forget also to ask "why" miss out on a lot of information. They focus on what candidates did, but not on what their motivations and reasoning were.

Asking "why" can help you learn more about candidates' previous responsibilities and how they dealt with them, about what they've learned, and about their accomplishments.

Arlene is interviewing Luke for the position of systems developer. Some of the main job requirements are the ability to write diagnostic programs and design and write code for operating systems and software. Follow along as Arlene interviews Luke.

Arlene: Do have you experience working on a team?

Luke: Yes, I did at my previous job as IT consultant, as well as outside work. I play basketball which has taught me how important it is to work as a team if you want to get results.

Arlene: Oh that's nice. Who do you play for?

Luke: I play for the Barunny Tigers.

Arlene: I have a couple of friends who play for a rival team. They really enjoy the sport and it's something that

I've always considered trying. Anyway, do you manage your time well?

Luke: Yes, I do.

Arlene: OK, and you have experience fixing problems with computers? Luke: Yes, definitely.

Question

For which reasons are Arlene's questions ineffective?

Options:

1. She diverges from the job requirement that she needs to find out about
2. She asks close-ended questions
3. She fails to ask why the candidate is qualified for the position
4. She focuses too much on the skills Luke needs to fulfill the job requirements
5. She doesn't ask clear questions

Answer:

Option 1: This option is correct. Arlene diverges from the topic when she starts asking about Luke's basketball activities. Instead, she should be spending her time asking questions that are directly relevant to the job requirements.

Option 2: This is a correct option. Arlene fails to ask open-ended question and therefore only gets simple "yes" or "no" answers, which don't tell her whether Luke meets the job requirements.

Option 3: This option is correct. By asking ineffective questions, Arlene fails to ask why Luke would or would not meet the job requirements. Arlene should have asked open-ended questions about Luke's experience with writing diagnostic programs and designing and writing code.

Option 4: This is an incorrect option. It's important to focus on job-related requirements to find out whether Luke will be able to fulfill them.

Option 5: This option is incorrect. All of Arlene's questions are clear, but they either go off on a tangent unrelated to the job requirements, are close ended, or fail to find out the why behind the whats.

Three main strategies can help you avoid asking ineffective interview questions. Prepare some questions in advance to guide you as you move through the interview. Use the job description for the position that's available to check that all the questions relate directly to actual job requirements. And finally, be flexible – let what the candidate tells you spark new questions.

Talking too much

Another common error interviewers make is talking too much instead of listening. You might feel you have a lot to tell a candidate about your company, your role there, and the position that's available. But remember that your main purpose in an interview is to get information from the candidate. How else are you going to find out whether the candidate is suitable for the position?

Along with talking too much about the company or themselves, interviewers sometimes put words in a candidate's mouth.

For example, an interviewer might say something like "So you feel that communication is important." This is leading and encourages agreement, rather than allowing expression of the candidate's own thoughts or feelings.

Another trap related to talking too much is spending too much time building rapport at the beginning of the interview.

Oliver uses the same structure during his interviews for a marketing representative position. Some of the main job requirements are a background in customer research and knowledge of developing customer proposals. Follow along as Oliver interviews Rose.

Oliver: So, Rose, are you familiar with how we market our products?

Rose: I know you use radio advertising and promotional deals.

Oliver: Yes, that's correct. We also keep a close eye on our competitors and conduct a lot of market and customer research. This is a very competitive and dynamic industry.

Rose: Right. I have some experience of conducting research.

Oliver: Yes, so currently there are 23 of us in marketing and we all work closely as a team. We also have regular meetings with the Research and Development Department to let our colleagues know what's going on with our customers.

Rose: Yes, I understand. That sounds good.

Oliver tends to dominate the conversation and neglects to listen to Rose.

As a result, he won't get the required information from Rose to help him make a fair assessment of her suitability for the position.

You can improve your listening when you're conducting an interview by following a couple of simple steps.

You can remind yourself that your role is to get the candidate speaking and to find out how well this person could perform the job that's available. Remember, around 80% of the questions you ask should be about the candidate's work experience as it relates to job requirements.

You can also make sure you take active interest in the candidate, listen carefully, and take notes when necessary.

Question

Three common errors interviewers make include failing to prepare properly, asking ineffective questions, and talking too much.

Match each example to the corresponding type of error. More than one example may match to a type of error.

Options:

A. Sarah focuses on what's in the candidate's resume, having only a vague idea about the requirements for the job

B. Joel asks candidates for a librarian position if they can use the most recent library management software without requesting more detail

C. Well into an interview for a copy editor position, Nicole asks several questions about a candidate's hobby

D. Jack gives details about the company for 25 minutes and spends the remaining ten minutes finding out about the candidate's work experience

Targets:

1. Lack of preparation
2. Asking ineffective questions
3. Talking too much

Answer:

Sarah hasn't prepared properly for the interview because she doesn't know the requirements of the job.

Joel asks a closed-ended question, which is ineffective because it doesn't elicit much information. Nicole's questions are also ineffective because they're not relevant to the position of copy editor.

Jack makes the error of talking too much during an interview. To make an effective judgment about the candidate's suitability for the job, he needs to talk less and listen more.

Not controlling the interview

A further common error is failing to stay in charge of an interview. This can mean that the discussion moves to irrelevant topics.

Or it could mean there is an imbalance in your focus – too much time is spent on some issues and too little on others.

As the interviewer, it's your job to control an interview, making sure it flows the way you want it to. You should aim to spend an appropriate amount of time discussing each relevant area of the candidate's background and skills.

Staying in control also means you're able to get candidates back on track when they are spending too long on a particular issue or discussing a topic that's not relevant.

For example, what if you're interviewing for the position of sales representative and a candidate tends to focus on his work years ago as a marketing assistant?

You need to guide the candidate back so that he talks more about the recent sales experience described on his resume.

Keeping control

In order to know which issues to cover in an interview and roughly how much time you should allow for each of these, you need to have read the candidate's resume and the job description. In other words, your ability to guide an interview effectively will depend on the preparation you do beforehand.

These techniques can help you keep control of an interview:

- balancing the time allocated for the interview to ensure all important areas are covered, without the interview becoming too long,
- interrupting appropriately if the candidate becomes side-tracked, and
- following a planned interview strategy.

Gavin is interviewing Carrie for the position of architect in his construction company. He plans to spend time on each job requirement – including ten minutes on the ability to work within a budget, ten minutes on negotiating skills, and five minutes on client relations. Gavin sticks to his plan by using polite interruptions and changes of topics.

In the interview with Carrie, Gavin demonstrates good control.

Gavin makes sure he has planned his time in advance so that he doesn't get stuck on discussing just one job requirement.

He doesn't rush Carrie, but he also doesn't let the interview drag on. And when necessary, he tactfully interrupts her and uses a change of subject to stick to his interview plan.

Failing to challenge assumptions

A final mistake many interviewers make is failing to challenge their own assumptions. It's very easy to judge candidates based on first impressions. But these initial judgments can make you biased, which means you may not listen carefully to the candidate or you may end up making an inappropriate hiring decision.

To challenge your own assumptions, you have to be aware of your own bias. There are several types of bias you should avoid during interviews, including first impression bias, similarity bias, halo bias, time pressure bias, and contrast bias.

See each type of bias to find out what to watch out for when you're conducting interviews.

First impression bias

How do you "size up" someone you've just met? Is the person attractive or plain? Friendly or shy? Consciously or not, people make snap judgments based on subtle cues. They then tend to overlook information that contradicts their first impressions. Interviewers need to make an effort to overcome this type of bias.

Similarity bias

Which candidate is best suited for a position in sales – the one who talks with a New Zealand accent or the one with the Canadian accent? It probably depends on whether one of them sounds like you. Interviewers may overemphasize the good qualities in candidates who are most similar to them.

Halo bias

A great salesperson doesn't always turn into a great, or even competent, sales manager. When a candidate has great credentials in one area, an interviewer may judge that candidate more generously than others. Similarly, someone weak in just one area may be judged more harshly. This is known as halo bias.

Time pressure bias

How much time can you invest in conducting interviews? If you feel an urgent need to fill a position, you may be less critical when evaluating candidates. And when the pressure is on to make a decision, everyone may look like a good candidate.

Contrast bias

You've just suffered through six interviews. No one had the skills or the personality for the job. Be cautious. Contrast bias can make the next candidate look like a winner by comparison, even if this person is only a little better qualified for the job than the rest.

Andrew knows it's critical that his company hire a new salesperson as soon as possible. Follow along as he interviews Glen.

Andrew: What did you do at the recruitment agency?

Glen: I was a researcher there. I was required to know a lot about different markets and to research different industries, companies, and people.

Andrew: Right, very good. Did you ever have to present individual reports?

Glen: Well, we produced reports as a team in the Research Department.

Andrew: That's fine. We can always teach you how to present reports. So, what sales experience do you have?

Glen: I don't have any sales experience but my position at the recruitment agency gave me the opportunity to find out about the skills and responsibilities of the position of salesperson. I did a lot of research in this area.

Andrew: OK. We have a training program that we put new employees through, and I'm sure you'll learn easily.

In the interview, it's obvious that time pressure is affecting Andrew's judgment. He seems biased in the candidate's favor, despite several indications that Glen lacks the experience and skills for a job in sales.

Three strategies can help you challenge your own assumptions about candidates:

- pause for a moment and make a mental list of your observations, making an effort to put them aside – doing this may help you to remain positive and open-minded,
- plan key questions before the interview and ask candidates these questions – that way you'll use the same words each time because even subtle variations can give one candidate an edge, and
- use the same format for all interviews, which will also help ensure that no candidate gets an unmerited advantage over another.

Question

Jackie is interviewing Tom, a candidate for a job as a statistician. She instantly takes a liking to Tom and everything he says seems to please her. She asks questions related to the job requirements and interprets his answers positively – even when they don't match with the job specifications. When Tom redirects the interview to talk about his previous work as a math teacher, Jackie enjoys the anecdotes about the school children.

What errors does Jackie make during this interview?

Options:
1. She fails to challenge her assumptions
2. She fails to control the interview effectively
3. She asks ineffective questions
4. She talks too much

Answer:

Option 1: This is a correct option. Jackie takes an instant liking to Tom and interprets everything he says positively. Jackie is showing first impression bias. She may also be affected by similarity bias, judging Tom more favorably because she happens to share his interests outside work.

Option 2: This option is correct. Jackie allows Tom to redirect the interview and talk about a topic that is unrelated to the job at hand.

Option 3: This is an incorrect option. Jackie does ask job-related questions. The trouble is she is not listening to the answers carefully enough because she has formed a too favorable first impression that may be clouding her judgment.

Option 4: This option is incorrect. Jackie seems to allow Tom to answer her questions and talk about his time as a math teacher. She probably needs to do a little more talking to redirect the interview.

The five most common interviewing errors are failing to prepare properly in advance, asking ineffective questions, talking too much instead of listening, not staying in control of the interview, and failing to challenge personal assumptions.

Being aware of these errors can help you avoid them and so ensure the interviews you conduct are effective.

AVOID UNFAIR PRACTICES

Avoid unfair practices

Legal issues

The last thing any company needs is a lawsuit brought against it for unfair hiring practices. As someone who interviews job candidates, you have a role to play in ensuring this doesn't happen. It's essential you're aware of potentially controversial issues as you prepare for interviews, so you don't act unfairly.

The interview process should be an objective one that follows formal guidelines for assessing job candidates' suitability. Sometimes though, interviewers may be unfair – and even violate employment laws – without realizing they're doing this.

This topic will give you an overview of some of the main legal concerns you should watch out for as you prepare to interview job candidates.

Employment legislation that deals with the hiring process differs from country to country, so it's important that you familiarize yourself with the relevant legislation in your country.

It's also important to keep up to date with this legislation, which may change regularly, and to seek the advice of legal professionals if anything is unclear.

The main legal issues for interviewers to consider relate to four areas of concern:
- discrimination,
- promises,
- testing, and
- nepotism.

See each area of concern for an overview of how it relates to the interviewing process.

Discrimination

As an interviewer, you're legally entitled to ask job candidates questions that relate directly to their suitability for a job.

However, asking questions related to race, gender, religion, national origin, disability, marital status, or sexual orientation is considered discriminatory.

Promises

Some interviewers may make, or imply, promises to interviewees on behalf of their companies. If the promises made aren't realistic and therefore aren't fulfilled, interviewees may hold the companies legally accountable for breaking them.

Making promises also raises legal issues if these promises don't comply with the employment laws of your country.

Testing

Employers may want job applicants to undergo various types of tests. These can include aptitude, psychological, and personality tests, as well as various medical and drug tests.

However, employment laws in many countries impose restrictions on the circumstances in which these tests may be used.

Nepotism

Nepotism refers to the practice of favoring family or friends in employment decisions. Although it's acceptable to interview and hire relatives or friends, laws in many countries make it illegal to favor them unfairly over other job applicants.

The consequences for companies of unfair or illegal interviewing practices can be severe. For example, they can include expensive lawsuits, fines, court-ordered financial settlements, and damage to the company's reputation.

Avoiding questions and actions that are unfair or illegal during interviews has two main benefits. It helps ensure you and your company avoid legal penalties and it can improve the effectiveness of your hiring choices.

See each benefit to find out more about it.

Avoid legal penalties

By asking only appropriate questions and assessing candidates fairly, you help ensure you don't violate employment laws. You also make it less likely that candidates you interview will find cause to bring legal cases against you or your company, or that there's any grounds for these cases.

Increase effectiveness of hiring

Acting fairly and legally involves assessing all candidates based strictly on their abilities to do a job, without factoring in unrelated criteria. Doing this makes it more likely you'll hire the person who's best suited to a position.

Question

Solomon keeps up to date with the legislation surrounding hiring and makes sure that he adheres to fair practices when interviewing candidates.

Which are benefits that Solomon will realize from knowing the legal issues surrounding hiring?

Options:

1. He'll be more effective when interviewing candidates
2. He'll be able to use legal terminology during interviews
3. He'll avoid financial and other penalties
4. He can make promises to candidates regarding company benefits

Answer:

Option 1: This is a correct option. By remaining aware of and up-to-date with legal issues, you'll know the importance of focusing on job-related issues during the interview. This focus will help you find a suitable candidate for the job – one who demonstrates job-related skills and experience.

Option 2: This is an incorrect option. The point of knowing the legal issues surrounding hiring is not to increase your legal vocabulary. Rather, it gives you the knowledge you need to avoid penalties, and helps make you a more effective interviewer.

Option 3: This option is correct. By contravening certain legislation relating to hiring, you may be liable for a financial, or other, penalty. Knowing about hiring legislation, therefore, can help you avoid expensive lawsuits that may affect your productivity.

Option 4: This option is incorrect. Knowing the legal issues surrounding hiring means that you will avoid making promises to candidates, who may hold you liable to those promises if hired.

Discrimination

The most important guideline for avoiding discrimination in interviews is to ensure all questions you ask are based on an established set of job-specific requirements.

You should avoid asking candidates questions that aren't directly related to whether their skills, qualifications, and experience make them suitable for a particular job.

For instance, asking if a candidate for a managerial position has children has no direct bearing on this person's capacity to perform the job. If the position is awarded to someone else, the candidate could use the question against you as evidence of discrimination.

Other questions to avoid include "Are you physically fit?" "What's your marital status?" "What's your birth date?" and "Have you ever been arrested?" Unless they clearly indicate an ability or inability to perform a task – for example, a firefighter must be physically fit – such questions are considered discriminatory. This is so because it's possible you might use them to exclude certain candidates based on criteria unrelated to a job's real requirements. For example, you could exclude candidates with health problems or above a certain age. Such actions are potentially illegal.

Sometimes candidates you interview may volunteer information that's not job-related. Did you know that even if you didn't ask a discriminatory question, this can have legal implications?

Say you mention to a candidate for a managerial position that the job often requires after-hours work. The candidate then explains she has two children and an ailing mother who stays with her.

If this candidate doesn't get the job, she may claim discrimination on the basis of the personal information she gave you.

If applicants give you non-job-related information that could be viewed as discriminatory, it's important you respond appropriately:
- make sure you don't write down any of the personal information provided by the applicants,
- don't go into more detail about the information or ask questions about it, and
- inform applicants that the information provided is not job-related and that you'd like to focus purely on discussing their skills and qualifications.

Promises

As well as taking care to avoid discrimination during interviews, you shouldn't make or imply a promise you know you won't be able to honor. In particular, never raise an applicant's hopes unfairly or give an applicant a false sense of security.

For instance, an interviewer may exaggerate how well the company is doing and promise its success will only increase in the near future.

The candidate offered the job may accept it, partly because of this positive promise. But what happens if five months later, the company is facing financial problems and the individual is laid off?

This person could bring a lawsuit against the company.

The best way to avoid making false promises is to always tell candidates the truth. Being as truthful and accurate as you can helps avoid possible legal problems later.

It also helps ensure candidates form realistic expectations about the job during the interviews.

Question

Which promise do you think could cause legal trouble?

Options:

1. "If you get the job, you'll be working with other trainees for the first six weeks."

2. "We're in the business of hiring people, not firing them, so your job security is guaranteed."

3. "There may be times that you'll have to work after hours, but it's our policy to pay overtime."

Answer:

You can't guarantee an applicant's job security. If the company runs into financial, or other trouble, employees' jobs may be at risk. Promising job security gives applicants a false sense of security.

In essence, follow four rules to avoid making promises to job applicants:

- don't forecast your organization's future financial prospects,
- don't make approximations about the future value of your organization's stock options,
- avoid saying things that could hinder your right to make personnel decisions going forward – for

example, by stating that you don't fire employees who perform well, and
- be sure to provide an accurate description of the position being offered.

Testing

Properly developed and managed tests provide organizations with a methodical and objective method for screening applicants. They can help in finding the best people for jobs – those who have the relevant skills aren't likely to engage in illegal or counterproductive behavior and will respond well to training.

However, you want to make sure that any tests you ask applicants to take relate directly to the requirements for the job and that they follow relevant employment legislation.

It's also important to ensure any tests you conduct don't unfairly exclude any groups of individuals from consideration.

Remember, tests may be carefully examined if there is a belief that discrimination in employment decisions has occurred.

It could be that score differences in tests result in exclusionary effects on a group. The term "adverse impact" means that the selection rate of a given demographic group – for example, females vs. males – is substantially lower than the selection rate of the majority group.

Before you use a test, you need to check whether adverse impact might occur. You should also think about how to minimize any exclusionary effects, while maintaining the ability to make valid inferences based on test scores.

Nepotism

To prevent nepotism during interviewing and subsequent hiring decisions, an organization should develop and implement a nepotism policy. The policy should outline rules regarding the hiring of relatives and friends, as well as rules relating to employees who work for the same organization and get married.

During the interview process, you should treat family members and friends in the same manner as other job applicants.

So you should ask family members or friends the same questions you'd ask other job candidates, and you should check their references.

Also, if an applicant has relatives or friends already working for your company, you shouldn't allow this information to influence your selection decision.

Question

Which are ways to avoid unfair practices during interviews?

Options:

1. Ensure that questions posed to candidates don't relate to their religion

2. Don't provide a full description of the job to candidates

3. Don't promise candidates that they're likely to be hired

4. Ask questions during interviews to find out more about candidates' personal lives

5. Don't formulate your own pre-employment test aimed at evaluating a candidate's personality

6. Follow the same interview procedures for family and friends who are being considered for a job

Answer:

Option 1: This option is correct. Asking questions based on religion can be viewed as discriminatory and may lead to legal action. Typically, religion is not a job-related specification.

Option 2: This option is incorrect. Providing a full and accurate description of the job will help avoid candidates later claiming they were unaware the job entailed certain responsibilities. It will also help avoid the candidates having false expectations of what the job entails.

Option 3: This is a correct option. You should never make verbal or written promises to candidates that raise their hopes or expectations.

Option 4: This is an incorrect option. You shouldn't ask personal questions because these may be viewed as discriminatory, possibly resulting in a lawsuit against your company.

Option 5: This option is correct. Pre-employment tests should test job-specific criteria such as skills, and you should always confirm that any test is in line with employment legislation.

Option 6: This is a correct option. All candidates should be treated equally – you should ask the same questions and check the references of candidates who are family or friends.

Acting fairly and in accordance with employment legislation during interviews helps protect your organization against legal penalties, as well as improves hiring choices.

Areas of concern you should know to avoid when preparing for interviews include: asking discriminatory questions; making promises to applicants that you can't keep and that raise their expectations; implementing inappropriate or illegal forms of pre-employment testing; and nepotism – or showing favoritism to applicants who are family members or friends.

CHAPTER III - CONDUCTING AN EFFECTIVE INTERVIEW

CHAPTER III - Conducting an Effective Interview

In this book, you'll learn how to open an interview so that the candidate feels at ease and communicates openly with you. You'll also discover how to ask effective questions that are clear, thorough, and consistent, so you draw out all the information you need. Finally, you'll learn how to close an interview on a positive note, making sure you've covered everything.

Because part of the purpose of an interview is to help candidates decide whether they want to work for your organization, an effective interview should allow time for candidates to ask questions.

Also, remember that it's up to you, as a representative of your organization, to conduct yourself professionally during all phases of the interview process.

OPENING AN INTERVIEW

Opening an interview

Build rapport

Have you ever been to an interview where the interviewer was cold and unfriendly? If so, you probably became even more tense during the interview than you already were and felt less inclined to open up. Conversely, if an interviewer takes a few minutes to put you at ease, you're more likely to speak openly. So as an interviewer yourself, remember that an interview isn't an interrogation – it's a chance to get to know a job candidate.

Opening an interview properly is important because it sets the tone for the rest of the interview. You should build rapport with the candidate, explain the interview format – outlining what the candidate should expect, and then ask introductory questions before transitioning into the main part of the interview.

It's normal for a candidate to be nervous about an interview and this can make open communication difficult.

You can make the candidate feel comfortable by building rapport. Taking the time to do this at the outset is likely to result in a more productive interview.

It's also likely to leave the candidate with a more positive impression of your organization and of the position that's available.

To build rapport with a candidate, you should take these steps:
- greet the candidate warmly and introduce yourself,
- help the candidate acclimatize and settle comfortably into the interview environment, and
- use open, positive body language.

See each way of putting a candidate at ease for more information about it.

Greet the candidate

First you should greet the candidate warmly and by name, introduce yourself, and briefly explain your role in the organization.

For example, you might say "Hi Stacey. I'm Anna, the general manager here. I'm very pleased to meet you."

Help the candidate acclimatize

To help the candidate relax into the interview environment, you should guide this person to a comfortable seat and, if relevant, assist by offering a place for this person's belongings.

Also, if other people are in the room, explain who they are, their roles, and why they're there. For example, you might gesture to a seat and say "Please take a seat. May I take that coat for you? This is my colleague Peter Reed. He manages the division and will participate in the interview. "

Use positive body language

You should maintain positive, open body language throughout an interview, but especially at the outset when candidates are likely to be nervous. Smile, maintain direct eye contact to indicate your interest, and be friendly.

Also ensure your tone of voice is light, friendly, and warm. If your tone is uninterested or irritable, even a polite question like "Did you find the building easily?" is unlikely to put a candidate at ease.

At the start of an interview, you should encourage, not prohibit, small talk to break the ice. You should focus on a subject unrelated to the interview. For example, you might say "What do you think of this strange weather we're having?" or "The traffic always seems worse on rainy days – have you noticed that?"

Acknowledging the stress involved in interviews and using humor – provided it's appropriate – can help dispel tension.

However, be careful to avoid subjects that could make candidates uncomfortable, force them to take sides, or lead to in-depth conversation. For instance, avoid topics like sport, religion, and politics.

Although it's essential to make the candidate feel at ease, bear in mind that this opening stage shouldn't take more than a few minutes. You might even complete it while walking the candidate from a reception area to the interview room.

Question

Which are effective ways to build rapport with a candidate at the outset of an interview?

Options:

1. Chat briefly about neutral subjects that have nothing to do with the interview

2. Offer the candidate a place to sit and to put his or her belongings

3. Make a joke about how interviews can be stressful for both parties

4. Ask for the candidate's first impressions of your organization

5. Advise the candidate just to ignore the three other people sitting in on the interview

Answer:

Option 1: This option is correct. You can help set a candidate at ease by encouraging small talk about benign subjects that don't put the candidate on the spot.

Option 2: This is a correct option. In the interview room, you should direct the candidate to a comfortable seat and, if relevant, offer a safe place for this person's belongings. This will help the candidate acclimatize.

Option 3: This option is correct. Appropriate humor can help dispel tension and put a candidate at ease.

Option 4: This option is incorrect. A question related to your organization suggests that you're already testing the candidate. To build rapport, rather start with a question unrelated to the interview.

Option 5: This is an incorrect option. You should introduce any other people who will be participating in the interview process, and explain their roles, to set the candidate at ease.

Explain the interview format

After building rapport with the candidate, you should explain the interview's format so the candidate knows what to expect. This puts the candidate at ease and it establishes your control over the direction of the interview. Be open about the interview – what you'll cover and how long it will take.

For example, you might cover the following points:
- whether any other interviews or interviewers will be involved in the full interview process,
- the approximate length of the interviewk
- there'll be time for the candidate to ask questions, and
- you'll be taking notes for the duration of the interview.

By telling the candidate what to expect from the start, you establish control of the course an interview will take. Whatever format the interview will have, though, you should ensure the way you explain your approach does set a positive note and puts the candidate at ease. You should also give the candidate a chance to ask any questions.

Follow along as Janice, Tom, and Mary explain the different types of interview formats they use when opening an interview.

Janice: "Good morning. I'm Janice, the HR manager. I'll be interviewing you for the sales representative position. I'll be asking you some questions about your experience, and then I'll explain how the organization works and what the position requires. Finally I'll answer any questions you may have. Is there anything you'd like me to clarify before we start?" - *says Janice warmly*.

Tom: "Hey there. I'm Tom, the manager for this department. So you're applying for the sales rep job, huh? Great. Well, I'm sure you've got lots of questions, but I'll start off by telling you a bit about what we do here. Then we'll talk about whether you think you're up for it! Is that OK?" - *says Tom, friendly and warmly.*

Mary: "Hi. I'm Mary. Nice to meet you. Today you'll have to answer some questions about your experience and qualifications. You should know the format for interviews so I won't go into the details. Let's get started." - *says Mary with a formal and unfriendly tone.*

Select each photo of the interviewers for more information about their approaches to opening an interview.

Janice

Janice's approach is very structured and formal, but her warm tone and open body language keeps this from being unfriendly. She ensures the candidate knows exactly what to expect from the remainder of the interview.

Tom

Tom's approach is very casual, but he conveys confidence about his ability to maintain control of the interview. He gives the candidate an idea of what will be involved and an opportunity to ask questions.

Mary

Mary's approach is likely to put the candidate on edge. She uses "you" language which can sound accusatory, doesn't explain her role in the organization, has an unfriendly tone, and only makes a brief description of the interview format. She also doesn't ask if the candidate has any questions about the format.

Question

Which are effective ways to explain the format of an interview to a candidate?

Options:

1. State that you'll first describe the position, then ask questions, and finally answer the candidate's questions

2. State that during the interview, you'll be testing how the candidate responds to your questions

3. Challenge the candidate to take the initiative and decide what this person thinks is most important to cover during the interview

Answer:

Option 1: This is the correct option. It summarizes the main interview stages so the candidate knows what to expect and can relax.

Option 2: This is an incorrect option. Stating you'll be testing the candidate will only make the candidate more nervous. Also, it's already obvious that during an interview, you'll assess the candidate. Instead, be clear and open about what course the interview will take so the candidate knows what to expect.

Option 3: This option is incorrect. By explaining the format you want to take in the interview, you establish your control and put the candidate at ease. If you ask the candidate to decide on the direction of the interview, you may end up making this person uneasy. Moreover, you may not get the information you need to establish whether the candidate is suitable for the job.

Introductory questions

After building rapport and explaining what the interview will cover, you might ask a few introductory questions to ease the candidates into the interview – you want to get them talking and feeling at ease when doing so. This is particularly appropriate for candidates that seem overly nervous.

You should ask about subjects the candidate will be familiar with and find easy to talk about. For example, you could ask about a hobby or an interesting job the candidate held in the past.

Your questions should be open-ended to encourage the candidate to talk, but not so broad that the candidate doesn't know where to start.

You may be tempted to leave it up to candidates to talk about themselves, but this could make them even more tense at a time when you should be helping them relax. Some classic mistakes are saying "Tell me about yourself" or "I didn't read your resume – can you fill me in?" It's also a mistake to summarize what's on the candidate's resume – for example, saying something like "I see you majored in computer science."

See each example of what not to say in an interview for more information about why it would be stressful for a candidate.

"Tell me about yourself."

Asking candidates to tell you about themselves puts them on the spot – where should they start and what is it you want to hear about?

The candidates might also give you irrelevant information or information you aren't entitled to obtain – for example, about their religious beliefs or marital status.

"I didn't read your resume – can you fill me in?"

Indicating that you didn't bother to prepare for an interview will give candidates a negative impression of you and your organization. The candidates also won't know where to start or how much detail to go into.

"I see you majored in computer science."

If you tell candidates something they've already made clear on their resumes, they may not know how to respond. Do you want that person to elaborate, explain their choices, or merely confirm the facts?

Rather ask a more specific, open-ended question, like "What did you enjoy about studying computer science?"

Question

Asking introductory questions at the start of an interview can help put candidates at ease.

What should you do at this stage?

Options:

1. Ask candidates about topics they'll want to talk about
2. Avoid simply repeating facts on candidates' resumes
3. Ask broad questions about candidates' histories
4. Avoid questions related to candidates' personal interests

Answer:

Option 1: This option is correct. You can get candidates talking by asking them specific questions about topics they're interested in and that they'll know how to answer.

Option 2: This is a correct option. If you simply repeat what's on candidates' resumes, it's likely the candidates won't know how to respond.

Option 3: This option is incorrect. You should avoid asking candidates questions so broad they don't know where to start or what information you're expecting in response.

Option 4: This is an incorrect option. Asking about an interest a candidate has is a good way to get this person talking.

Opening an interview

Theresa is a project manager at an advertising company where James has applied for a job as a graphic designer. James recently graduated from college and doesn't have much work experience – and he's very nervous about the interview.

Follow along as Theresa tries to help James relax at the opening of the interview.

Theresa: Hi James. Welcome! I'm Theresa, a project manager here. - *Theresa says warmly.*

James: Hi Theresa. It's very nice to meet you. - *James says, formally.*

Theresa: Great day out there, isn't it? - *Theresa says warmly.*

James: Yeah. - *James is nervous*

Theresa: Right, so just to give you an idea of what to expect here today - this will probably take about an hour and a half. I'll start by asking you some questions. Then we'll talk about what we do here and what the position would involve. And finally you'll have an opportunity to ask anything you'd like to know about the company. Sound good? - *Theresa is smiling.*

James: Yes, yes, that sounds fine. - *James is still nervous.*

Theresa: So you ...you've.. finished college? - *Theresa is clearly not quite prepared and is looking at James' resumé.*

James: You mean graduated? - *James is taken aback.*

Theresa: Uh, yes. - *Theresa is friendly but still uncertain.*

James: Well, yeah. I mean, isn't having a degree a prerequisite for the job? - *James is questioning.*

Theresa: Yes, of course. Talk to me about your coursework. I see you minored in set design – what did you enjoy about that? - *Theresa asks more confidently.*

James: Oh that's easy! I love being creative and using my hands. And I grew up in a theatrical family, so it was a natural step for me... - *James says, relieved to have a foothold in the conversation.*

Theresa does a good job of calming James at the opening of the interview. She greets him warmly, introduces herself and her role at the company, and opens with some small talk. She follows up by explaining the interview format so that James knows what to expect.

However, she then refers to something obvious on his resume. James is uncertain about how to respond or thinks she's unprepared.

Theresa recovers and asks a more focused question about something James can speak about.

It's important to set a candidate at ease at the opening of an interview. To do this, you should build rapport, explain what format the interview will follow, and then ask introductory questions that don't relate directly to the interview to get the candidate relaxed and talking.

THE FUNCTIONS OF DIFFERENT QUESTION TYPES

The functions of different question types

Interview question types

The core of any interview is asking questions – and this is what you should spend about 85% of the allocated time doing. So it's vital that you ask effective questions. Otherwise, you won't get all the information you need to determine a candidate's suitability for a job.

You can divide interview questions into five main types: competency-based or behavioral situational or hypothetical open-ended close-ended, and probing

In addition to using these question types effectively, it's important to ask each candidate more or less the same questions in the same order. This ensures the interviewing process is fair and consistent.

Question
What do you think are benefits of knowing the functions of the different types of interview questions?
Options:

1. You'll be better able to draw out the information you need from candidates to make an effective hiring decision

2. You'll be able to complete interviews quickly

3. You'll be better able to maintain control of the interview

4. You'll be able to keep candidates on edge by switching the types of questions you use

Answer:

Knowing the functions of different types of questions enables you to elicit the information you need and maintain control over the interview by ensuring candidates won't spend time giving you irrelevant information.

So there are two main benefits to knowing when to use each of the question types. You'll be better able to get the information you need to make an effective hiring decision. And you'll find it easier to keep an interview on course.

Competency-based questions

Given that you can't look into the future, how can you assess whether candidates have what it takes to perform a specific job? One of the answers is to find out about how they dealt with specific situations in the past.

Competency-based questions focus on determining whether candidates have the required skills, or competencies, for a given position.

Typically, they ask for examples of how a candidate dealt with a specific problem or circumstance in the past. An example is "Can you tell me about a time when you had to deal with an unhappy client?"

Every job requires different competencies, but there are four main categories – tangible or technical, knowledge, behavior, and interpersonal skills.

See each type of competency to find out more about it.

Tangible

Tangible – or technical – competencies are easiest to demonstrate in practice because they relate to what a person can do.

Knowledge

Knowledge-based competencies relate to what people know and how they think. For example, you might want to find out what kind of problem-solving abilities and decision-making skills candidates have.

Behavior

Behavior-based competencies relate to how a person acts under certain conditions. For example, if a position requires a high level of customer retention, you might ask questions that indicate whether a candidate is committed to developing lasting partnerships with customers.

Interpersonal skills

Interpersonal skills determine how well someone interacts with other people. You might want to know how well candidates listen or whether they can maintain self-control when upset, for example.

Sometimes competency-based questions – derived directly from job requirements and focusing on the technical or tangible aspects of a job – may not give enough information.

If you need to know how candidates will work with a team, fit into the office culture, or work with a particular manager, you may need to ask more generic competency-based questions.

For example, you might ask a general question like "How did you manage a dispute that arose on your team?"

So it's best to avoid focusing on just one type of competency in the questions you ask. This is because all competencies combine to determine candidates' performances.

For example, a graphic designer may have excellent technical skills but lack interpersonal skills. This could mean the designer won't be able to work effectively with others and so isn't suitable for a position that requires a lot of interaction with clients.

Amrit has applied for the position of customer service agent at an Internet book supplier. Her resume's impressive and she's attending an interview with a division manager, Corbin.

Follow along as Corbin uses competency-based questions to find out more about Amrit.

Corbin: Tell me about a time in your previous job where you were faced with an unhappy customer. What happened and how did you handle it?

Amrit: I was working as a sales clerk when I had to deal with a gentleman who got very irate when he couldn't get the one he wanted.

Corbin: What did you do?

Amrit: I explained the situation to him, but he didn't care. He started shouting. I tried my best to be understanding. I let him blow off some steam.

Corbin: Weren't you worried he might become violent? Did you think of calling security? What was going through your head at the time?

Amrit: No, I've dealt with difficult customers before. I figured he was just another cranky old guy.

Corbin: So how did it end?

Amrit: After a while, I knew he wasn't going to stop, so I told him straight out he was being ridiculous and that I didn't have to stand for it. He walked out furious, but it was a relief for me.

Question

What did Corbin learn about Amrit through his competency-based questions?

Options:

1. How she handled a difficult customer in the past
2. Where she received training in customer service
3. What aspects of customer service she enjoys

Answer:

Option 1: This is the correct option. Corbin learned that when Amrit had to deal with a difficult customer in the past, she ended by being rude and unprofessional. This suggests she may lack required competencies for a customer service agent.

Option 2: This option is incorrect. Corbin could have obtained details of Amrit's training using different question types – or perhaps simply by reading her resume.

Option 3: This is an incorrect option. To find out this information, Corbin wouldn't need to focus on past behavior which is the reason competency-based questions are used.

In the interview, Corbin used competency-based questions to assess a specific example of Amrit's past performance.

Corbin knows it's unlikely Amrit will face exactly the same situation again. However, her descriptions of how she reacted in the past tell him a lot about how she's likely to handle difficult customers in the future.

Corbin's questions touch on all four competency types. They examine Amrit's tangible or practical ability to deal with a customer, her thought processes and behavior under the conditions specified in the question, and her ability to interact with people.

Understandably, candidates stress strengths and attributes, and interviewers tend to focus on the positive as they seek a good match for the job. As a result, interviewers may overlook relevant negative characteristics.

You should try to ask some competency-based questions that will give proof of past mistakes and problems. For example, you might ask "Tell me what you need to improve about yourself. Give an example of how this characteristic hindered your ability to achieve results in the past."

Question

For which purpose do you use competency-based questions in an interview?

Options:

1. To find out how a candidate performed in the past

2. To explore a candidate's career goals and how they relate to the available job

3. To get a general impression of a candidate's attitude to work

4. To find out how a candidate thinks or what problem solving abilities they have

Answer:

Option 1: This option is correct. Competency-based questions ask how a candidate dealt with specific situations in the past. The responses indicate the candidate's likely ability to meet specific job requirements in the future.

Option 2: This is an incorrect option. You use competency-based questions to review the competencies candidates have exhibited in the past, rather than to explore their goals for the future.

Option 3: This is an incorrect option. You use competency-based questions to review the competencies candidates have exhibited in specific examples of situations in the past.

Option 4: This option is correct. Competency-based questions can help you obtain key information about a person's technical or practical competencies, as well as competencies related to knowledge, behavior, and the ability to interact with others. The knowledge competency relates to how a person thinks – what decision-making or problem-solving skills they have, for example.

Hypothetical questions

Sometimes you'll interview candidates who have little or no relevant work experience, or a candidate's resume doesn't reveal whether the candidate has gone through an experience similar to the situation you want to ask about. In these situations, it can be useful to ask hypothetical questions. You can think of these as "What would you do if..." questions.

Hypothetical questions inquire about an anticipated course of action. Usually, they're worded like problems or obstacles to which candidates must devise theoretical solutions.

An example is "What would you do if someone reported a case of workplace harassment to you?"

Question

Which question is hypothetical?

Options:

1. What would you'd do if you caught a customer stealing?

2. What did you do to boost team morale when it reached a low point?

3. Can you describe how you prevented delays from affecting the project's success?

Answer:

The question "What you'd do if you caught a customer stealing? is hypothetical because it prompts candidates to describe what they might do in a fictitious, albeit realistic, scenario. The other questions are competency based.

You can often convert a competency-based question into a hypothetical one simply by changing its tense, from past to future.

But remember hypothetical questions focus on how candidates think rather than on facts about how they behaved in the past.

You can use them to assess candidates' ability to reason, as well as their thought processes, values, creativity, work attitudes, and approach to assignments.

You'll get important information from asking hypothetical questions, but don't expect "correct" answers. The candidates's answers will be based on how they think rather than on what they know.

Question

For which purposes would you use hypothetical questions in job interviews?

Options:
1. To find out how candidates approach their work
2. To elicit examples about candidates' prior work experience
3. To find out whether candidates have the required qualifications and technical expertise to do a job
4. To evaluate a candidate's reasoning ability

Answer:

Option 1: This is a correct option. By asking a person how they'd act in hypothetical situations, you can tell how they approach work.

Option 2: This option is incorrect. You would use competency-based questions to learn of examples of

4. Open-ended questions a candidate's prior work experience.

Option 3: This is an incorrect option. You should have an idea of a candidate's qualifications from their resume, but you can also get more information by asking competency-based questions.

Option 4: This option is correct. You can ask candidates how they'd respond to job appropriate situations using hypothetical questions that reveal their thought processes and reasoning skills.

Open-ended questions

Competency-based and hypothetical questions usually take the form of open-ended questions. Open-ended questions encourage candidates to speak.

They require thought and elaboration, rather than just one-word answers like yes or no. And they can often provide the starting point for a whole avenue of enquiry.

These are examples of open-ended questions:

- "What are your career goals and how are they compatible with this role?"
- "How have your past responsibilities prepared you for dealing with the challenges ahead?"
- "What is the biggest plus point about this position?"

Faye is attending an interview for the position of researcher in a university's Anthropology Department. Follow along as Dave conducts the interview with Faye.

Dave: Can you tell me about your past experience as a researcher?

Faye: I studied research methodologies at university. After that, I worked for the city municipality. I then became a researcher at a local community college.

Dave: What were you responsible for doing at the community college?

Faye: I conducted research for various lecturers and for several of the college's projects. For example, I collated data on its adult education programs.

Dave: Can you give me an example of an assignment when you had to cope with an abundance of useless data?

Faye: Yes. I was preparing a report on reasons for absenteeism in the college's community outreach programs. To complete my report on time, I had to start by quickly identifying and discarding what wasn't relevant.

Dave asks Faye two general open-ended questions and one competency-based question during the interview. Open-ended questions are useful because they elicit information for further discussion and questions. For example, the information Faye provides about her role at a community college helps Dave formulate an appropriate competency-based question about her ability to sort and collate data.

Question

What do you think are the potential drawbacks of open-ended questions?

Options:

1. Answers can be short of verifiable facts
2. They leave candidates little room to express themselves
3. Answers can be too general or irrelevant
4. Answers can be too short and not reveal enough information

Answer:

Option 1: This option is correct. A candidate may resort to self-aggrandizing rhetoric and leave out useful or verifiable information.

Option 2: This is an incorrect option. Close-ended questions don't allow expansive answers.

Option 3: This is a correct option. As open-ended questions often serve for a starting point for a whole monologue, it's easy for a candidate to go off topic.

Option 4: This option is incorrect. Close-ended questions call for limited answers and are often followed by open-ended or probing questions.

You can avoid too general and rambling answers from a candidate if you combine open-ended questions with other question types. For instance, you can follow up a vague response with a competency-based question that asks for tangible examples.

Also, if a candidate begins to waffle, you can interrupt politely and use a more focused question to steer the interview back on track. For example, you can rephrase a broad question like "What relevant work experience have you had?" as "What relevant work experience have you gained in the last three years?"

Close-ended questions

Open-ended questions may sometimes be followed by close-ended questions to help elicit further information. Close-ended questions require short, succinct answers, like "yes" or "no." You use them to obtain crucial information quickly and to confirm facts.

If you require confirmation, or a specific detail, you may ask the following questions: What is your salary expectation?

How much notice do you need to give in your current position? Did you finish the postgraduate qualification?

Close-ended questions are useful for giving an interviewer more control or for seeking clarification. They can also help nervous candidates open up.

See each aim to find out more about it.

Give interviewer control

If a candidate starts giving irrelevant information or talking off topic, and you need to regain control of the interview, you can do so with close-ended questions that steer the person back on track.

For example, if a candidate is talking too much about one job, you might ask "When did you leave that job?"

Seek clarification

You may need to clarify or verify information the candidate has presented in a previous answer. For example, you might ask "So drawing on what you've said so far, can I assume that you prefer working independently rather than as part of a team?"

In addition, if there is one issue that could terminate the interview, such as the absence of an important job requirement, then asking about it up front in a direct, close-ended way can get you the information you need to know quickly and succinctly.

Help candidates open up

As close-ended questions are easy to answer, they can help put nervous candidates at ease and allow them to acclimatize to the interview situation. A series of simple questions confirming facts can then lead to open-ended questions.

So use close-ended questions when you need to control the interview, clarify a point, or help candidates open up.

But don't use them as a substitute for open-ended or competency-based questions and never as the only question type in your interview.

Remember, you can convert a question that can be answered by a single word into an open-ended or a competency-based question.

For example, "Have you done a lot of presentations?" will give you a single-word answer, telling you little about the applicant's experience. The open-ended version is better but still doesn't tell you much: "What is your experience with presentations?" If you make this a competency-based question, however, you'll get a job-related, detailed response: "Tell me about a time when you had to give a presentation to a large audience. How did you prepare for it?"

You should avoid loaded or multiple choice questions, which are typically close-ended.

Not only do they encourage short answers, they may make a candidate feel inhibited – what if their response is

Essentials of Interviewing and Hiring

not among the options? Candidates shouldn't feel forced to choose between two or more alternatives.

A question like "How would you describe your style of leadership? Proactive, controlling, aloof, or involved?" can be rephrased as "How would you describe your leadership style? Give an example of how you applied this style in a recent work situation."

In addition, as a general rule, avoid asking candidates any leading questions. These usually require a "yes" or "no" answer, and give the impression the interviewer has a preferred answer.

In the example "Don't you think that most employees need to be ruled with an iron fist?" the wording reveals what reply the interviewer expects and the answer won't reveal anything substantive.

Question

Which are functions of close-ended questions?

Options:

1. They can be used to test a candidate's reasoning abilities

2. They can be used to uncover relevant work experience

3. They can be used to verify facts

4. They can be used to put a nervous candidate at ease at the start of an interview

Answer:

Option 1: This option is incorrect. You would use a knowledge based competency question or a hypothetical question to test a candidate's reasoning ability.

Option 2: This is an incorrect option. You would use competency-based questions to examine a candidate's work experience.

Option 3: This option is correct. You can use a close-ended question to verify a fact given as part of an answer to a competency-based or open-ended question.

Option 4: This is a correct option. By asking a series of close-ended questions at the start of an interview, you can acclimatize a candidate to the experience and put them at ease.

Probing questions

During an interview, you use probing questions to delve more deeply for additional information. They are followups to candidates' responses to other question types. You use such questions to find out candidates' reasons for something, to get the candidates to qualify or expand, or to substantiate what they've said.

See each purpose of asking probing questions to learn more.

Find out reasons

To ask the reason for a previous response, you might use short, probing questions like "Why?" "How?" or "When?"

Qualify or expand

You can use probing questions to get the candidate to qualify or expand on a previous response. For example, you might ask "What caused management to deny your request?" or "What happened after the presentation?"

Substantiate

You can use probing questions to prompt candidates to validate what they've said. For example, if a candidate mentions having done research for an Arts Department, you might use a probing question like "Can you give some examples of what you researched?"

Generally, you should avoid asking candidates long lists of probing questions. This may come across as an interrogation and result in making the candidate uncomfortable or defensive.

Question

What are the functions of probing questions?

Options:

1. They can be used to expand on the answer to a previous question

2. They can be used to uncover the reason for a candidate's past actions

3. They can be used to examine a candidate's thought processes

4. They can be used to steer a candidate back on track if necessary

Answer:

Option 1: This is a correct option. A follow-up probing question can get a candidate to expand on a point.

Option 2: This option is correct. You can ask a probing question to discover the reasons behind a candidate's past action.

Option 3: This option is incorrect. You would use a knowledge based competency question or hypothetical question to discover how a candidate thinks.

Option 4: This is an incorrect option. You would use close-ended questions to regain interview control and get back on topic.

Question

Match the examples of interview questions to the corresponding question types.

Options:

A. What experience have you had in handling customer complaints?

B. What did you do in your previous job when a customer complained?

C. What happened after you submitted the report?

D. What would you do if an angry customer phoned you to complain about a problem with a product?

E. Have you ever dealt with a customer complaint?

Targets:

1. Competency-based
2. Hypothetical
3. Open-ended
4. Close-ended
5. Probing

Answer:

Competency-based questions prompt candidates to explain how they dealt with specific examples of situations in the past.

A hypothetical question outlines a theoretical problem or situation, and asks how a candidate would respond to it.

An open-ended question prompts a candidate to elaborate, rather than to provide a simple answer such as "yes" or "no."

A close-ended question asks for a short answer, such as "yes" or "no."

Probing questions prompt candidates to provide more information about their previous responses to questions.

Types of interview questions include competency-based, hypothetical, open-ended, close-ended, and probing questions.

During interviews, each of the question types serves different purposes. Knowing when to use each type can help ensure you get the information you need from candidates, and so make effective hiring choices.

HOW TO END AN INTERVIEW

How to end an interview

Covering everything

Whereas some interviewers have trouble opening an interview, others aren't sure how to close one. How do you know when you have enough information? What should you tell the candidate? Sometimes it can be difficult to determine how and when you should start wrapping up an interview.

To close an interview effectively, you should first determine whether you've covered everything you need to know and backtrack if necessary. You should then tell the applicant what happens next.

To determine whether you've covered everything, you need to answer several questions:
- Do I know enough about the candidate's education and experience?
- Have I described the organization and the available position?

- Have I told the candidate about the salary, benefits, and growth opportunities associated with the available position?
- Did I give the candidate a chance to ask questions?

Importance of providing adequate information

In addition to you finding out about a candidate, interviews are an opportunity for the candidates to learn more about your company. In this way, they can decide whether the available job will suit them. If you give candidates enough information about what to expect, you lower the risk that employees you hire will become disgruntled later.

Too often, an interviewer assumes candidates will have done their own background research on the company offering the position.

But interviewers should take responsibility for giving candidates all the information they need to make informed decisions. For example, what salary and benefits are being offered? What exactly does the job involve? And what opportunities are there for promotions?

You'll lower turnover if candidates are armed with this information before they decide whether to accept a job.

As head of a music academy, Sharon is nearing the end of her interview with Michael, who's applying for a teaching position. She realizes at the end of the interview that she didn't ask him why he wanted to become a teacher to begin with.

Follow along as Sharon goes back to cover the area she forgot to explore earlier in the interview with Michael.

Sharon: Michael, we're almost finished with the interview, and thank you again for coming in today. But I just need to backtrack a bit. Tell me, what made you decide to be a teacher?

Michael: Actually Sharon, it's what I've always thought I'd be doing. My father was a very dedicated history teacher and my mother taught violin to school children at our home. Perhaps that's where my love of music originated too.

Near the end of her interview with Michael, Sharon mentally reviews what she's asked the candidate.

She then adds a question to cover an area she neglected earlier. In this way, she ensures she has the information she needs to form a full picture of the candidate's suitability.

You might also briefly summarize the key issues you discussed during the interview.

This can provide a sense of closure and enable you and the candidate to review any remaining action items required.

What happens next

Once you've made sure you've covered everything, you can tell the candidate what happens next. What you say to candidates depends on the nature of the position and your level of interest in them. But you should be sure to tell candidates approximately when they'll hear from you, whether additional interviews will be held, and what to do if they think of other questions they need to ask in the mean time.

After an interview is over, you may want to give the candidate your business card in case they do have further questions.

Or you may prefer to let your assistant or receptionist handle any calls first.

Before you end the interview, you should ask one last time whether the candidate has any questions.

And remember that no matter how you close the interview, you should be sure to do so on a positive note – whether you're likely to hire the candidate or not.

Now follow along as Sharon closes her interview with Michael.

Sharon: Thanks Michael. I have a few more interviews scheduled over the coming week, but I'll e-mail you by the end of next week to inform you if another meeting will take place or if your application was unsuccessful.

Sharon: In the meantime, if you think of any more questions, please don't hesitate to call or e-mail me. Here's my card.

Michael: Thanks Sharon. I look forward to hearing from you.

Question

Which examples illustrate how to close an interview effectively?

Options:

1. Gary asks himself whether he has all the information he needs and decides he does. So he asks Dee if she has any questions, and then tells her he'll be in touch later that week.

2. Lee realizes he hasn't told Jean about the benefits she'd receive and does so. He then gives her his card in case she has any further questions, and tells her that he'll be in touch within the next two weeks.

3. Zack asks Ira whether she has any further questions and then closes the interview by shaking her hand and showing her the way out.

4. Diane makes sure Bill has all the information about the company that he needs, he then says he needs to leave for an important meeting and asks the receptionist to show him the way out.

Answer:

Option 1: This option is correct. Gary makes sure he's received and provided all the necessary information and lets Dee know what happens next.

Option 2: This is a correct option. Lee checks whether he's covered everything, corrects his omission, makes sure Jean can ask further questions if she needs to, and indicates when she'll hear from him.

Option 3: This option is incorrect. Zack checks whether Ira has any questions, but should let her know when she'll be contacted or give some indication of what happens next.

Option 4: This is an incorrect option. Diane checks that Bill has no further questions, but should let him know what happens next. Also, the interview doesn't end on a very positive note.

Although it doesn't take long, closing an interview properly is an important step. It's vital to make sure that you've covered everything you need to – and to backtrack if necessary. Once you've done this, you should tell the candidate what to expect next, including when this person will hear from you again.

CHAPTER IV - BEHAVIORAL INTERVIEW TECHNIQUES

CHAPTER IV - Behavioral Interview Techniques

In this chapter, you'll learn about the essentials of behavioral interview techniques:
- the definition of behavioral-based interviewing and this technique's benefits,
- how to develop questions for the behavioral-based interview, and
- how to use behavioral-based questions in practice.

BEHAVIORAL-BASED INTERVIEWING

Behavioral-based interviewing

Too often, interviewers focus on whether a candidate has the technical and functional skills and knowledge for a position, and forget to consider whether a candidate can demonstrate the competencies for the job. This can result in poor hiring decisions.

Bob needs to hire a production manager for a television show. After interviewing several candidates, he decides to appoint Luke. Of all the candidates, Luke has the most experience – more than what's required for the position.

He has a thorough knowledge of the technical processes involved in television production, including camera, lighting, sound, and editing. Luke also knows about the necessary licenses and clearances, and how to comply with regulations relating to liability and indemnity when shooting at different locations.

But after hiring him, Bob discovers that Luke can't manage the inevitable conflicts that arise among the many different people involved in the show. He lacks diplomacy and sensitivity, and the team's morale and commitment to the show decrease dramatically.

What went wrong?

Bob didn't interview Luke based on the competencies for success in the position, which include conflict management and building a high-performance team.

When you identify and define competencies, and then interview against them along with the technical and functional requirements, you increase your chances of finding someone who'll be successful in the position. Interviewing against competencies is the backbone of behavioral-based interviewing.

A competency is a behavior or set of behaviors describing the expected performance in a particular work context – for example, in the Accounting Department or as a senior manager.

Competencies are different from the other requirements for a particular job, such as technical skills, functional skills, and knowledge, education, and experience.

For example, a position might require three years of management experience, or three years of management experience developing teams within an organization. In the second situation, the interviewer seeks a candidate with three years of management experience coupled with a demonstrated competency of building effective teams.

So behavioral-based interviewing moves beyond asking questions centered on what's on a candidate's resume. At one time, this was a common approach – called the biographical approach – in which an interviewer worked through a candidate's resume, asking questions where relevant.

Behavioral-based interviewing instead focuses on asking how the candidate dealt with specific, relevant situations in the past.

The aim is to determine whether the candidate demonstrates the competencies required for the job. Many candidates may look good on paper, but when it comes to asking them how they fulfilled their roles, they offer little of substance.

Behavioral-based interviewing has three key characteristics:
- it investigates candidates' past performance as a predictor of their future performance,
- it focuses on identifying whether candidates have the required competencies for a position, and
- it minimizes bias by focusing on asking for facts about candidates' past performance.

Question

Based on these characteristics, what do you think are benefits of behavioral-based interviewing?

Options:

1. You're likely to complete interviews faster because you stay focused 2. You'll be more accurate in predicting candidates' abilities to do a job 3. You'll always elicit complete and truthful responses from candidates 4. You'll find it easier to avoid asking illegal or inappropriate questions

Answer:

Option 1: This option is incorrect. Behavioral-based interviewing isn't faster than other types of interviewing. It involves asking a series of questions to probe for information about candidates' responses in particular situations. The questions may elicit very detailed responses that trigger further questions.

Option 2: This option is correct. Behavioral-based interviewing enables you to evaluate candidates' past responses to real situations. It's fact-based and focused on required competencies, so it can help ensure you evaluate candidates' abilities to do a job and helps you predict whether they'll be successful at it. This leads to better hiring decisions.

Option 3: This option is incorrect. Behavioral-based interviewing can help keep both the interviewer and the person being interviewed focused on what's relevant by concentrating on the competencies required for a job. However, it can't ensure that candidates' responses are always complete and truthful.

Option 4: This option is correct. Behavioral-based interviewing involves focusing on the competencies candidates have demonstrated in real, job-related situations. This helps ensure you don't ask questions unrelated to candidates' abilities to perform the job for which you're interviewing.

Because behavioral-based interviewing involves evaluating whether candidates have the competencies they need to do a job, it can lead to more accurate candidate evaluations. The emphasis is kept on who has what it takes to perform the job well in practice.

This leads to better hiring decisions, which in turn can mean increased productivity, lower turnover, higher morale, and better quality employees for your department and organization.

It also means that the questions you ask relate directly to job performance. This helps ensure you ask only questions that are both appropriate and legal, rather than ones that stray from what is relevant or fair to ask job candidates.

Past performance

When you carry out a behavioral-based interview, you ask questions to gather information about how candidates dealt with specific, real situations in the past.

For example, an interviewer might ask candidates to describe a recent situation in which they had to rely on the cooperation of peers to get a job done.

It helps to find out about recent behavior, because it's this behavior that's likely to be repeated.

In general, traditional interview questions like "What are your greatest strengths and weaknesses?" or "What did you enjoy best about your last position?" tend to be weak, because it's likely candidates will have canned answers for them. They'll know what you want to hear.

And questions like "If you could be an animal, what would you choose to be?" – which some interviewers use – leave things wide open for the candidates and make the selection process less objective.

Such questions have nothing to do with the candidate's ability to do the job and can waste precious time in an interview.

Question

Which do you think are advantages of using a traditional interview format?

Options:

1. People know it and are therefore comfortable with it

2. It allows for many questions to be asked in a relatively short period of time

3. Some traditional questions can demonstrate a candidate's fit with the position

4. Questions like "Who are your heroes?" can provide important insights about a candidate

5. Traditional questions always reveal a candidate's fit with the competencies required for the job

Answer:

Option 1: This option is correct. One advantage of the traditional interview structure is that people are comfortable with it because it's familiar. This helps put candidates at ease.

Option 2: This option is correct. Many traditional interview questions call for relatively short answers. For example, a question like "What are your strengths?" will not take as long to answer as a question about how candidates showed initiative during the last project they worked on.

Option 3: This option is correct. Asking candidates to describe their ideal jobs or bosses may reveal whether the candidates will fit in with the prospective organization.

Option 4: This option is incorrect. Any insights that an interviewer claims to get from such questions are really just based on conjecture and supposition.

Option 5: This option is incorrect. Candidates are more familiar with traditional interview questions, and many books and web sites provide the "right" answers to typical interview questions. While preparing for their interviews, candidates can create perfect answers to each of these questions. Whether they're demonstrating competency for the job is not always clear, however.

Situational interview questions are similar to behavioral ones, but are hypothetical – they ask "What would you do if...?" These questions can provide useful information about how a candidate thinks. But a basic problem is that people don't always do what they say they would. Behavioral-based interview questions avoid this problem by focusing on the facts surrounding real situations.

Still, there's no way to know for sure how someone will behave in the future. But knowing how a candidate behaved in relevant situations in the recent past can give you a good idea. It enables you to assess whether job candidates have the required competencies – in other words, the ability to apply needed skills in practice.

So in a behavioral-based interview, it's important to get specific examples of how candidates behaved in the past. This ensures you're asking for facts, rather than candidates' impressions or opinions, and that your hiring decision will be based on these facts.

For example, you might ask "Can you tell me about a specific instance in which you disagreed with a customer?"

A question like "How do you deal with difficult customers?" is less effective because it's more general. Rather than calling for straight facts, it encourages candidates to tell you what they think you want to hear.

Question

Which do you think are effective examples of questions that will elicit relevant information about past performance?

Options:

1. How did you deal with multitasking on the last project you worked on?

2. What is your greatest weakness?

3. Can you tell me about a time when you disagreed with something a manager wanted you to do?

4. Have you ever felt stressed at work?

Answer:

Option 1: This is a correct option. This is an effective behavioral-based question because it asks for a recent, real-life example. It's specific, getting the candidate to provide details about a particular situation.

Option 2: This option is incorrect. This is not an effective behavioral-based question because it doesn't elicit specific information from candidates regarding past behavior or actions. It's a traditional interview question that candidates prepare for, and thus won't reveal if the candidate is suitable or not.

Option 3: This option is correct. In this example, candidates are asked to recall a specific, real situation that occurred in the past. This will provide the interviewer with useful information about how the candidates handled the situation.

Option 4: This is an incorrect option. This is not an effective behavioral-based question. The candidates can answer "yes" or "no" and avoid providing specific information regarding past experiences or situations.

Identifying competencies

The questions you ask about past behavior need to be focused on the relevant competencies for the job. It makes little sense asking a question about past behavior that's not relevant for the job at hand.

By asking questions related to the behaviors that will lead to the expected performance in a particular work context, you can assess how well a job candidate is likely to perform in a particular job.

So before holding behavioral-based interviews, you need to determine what competencies are required for the given job. The four main categories of competencies are those related to tangible or technical skills, knowledge, behavior, and interpersonal skills.

See each category of competency for more information about it.

Tangible or technical skills

Tangible or technical skills are critical for success in many positions. These concrete skills – such as the ability to apply technical expertise to problem solving or understanding relevant technologies – are important and should be explored during an interview. But a person can bring more than measurable skills to a job, and that's why the other competency categories also need to be explored.

For example, a candidate with excellent technical competencies but who's unable to communicate well with clients is unlikely to make a good IT technician.

Knowledge

The knowledge category refers to what a candidate knows and how this person thinks. These qualities are more difficult to measure than tangible skills, but are just as important.

Knowledge competencies typically required of an IT technician, for example, include skills in identifying, interpreting, and solving problems – as well as up-to-date knowledge about computer systems. A lawyer needs the legal competencies to provide appropriate and up-to-date legal advice and counsel.

Behavior

Finding out about behavioral competencies can make a dramatic difference in how you view two candidates with similar technical abilities. This type of competency relates to a candidate's ability to behave appropriately in different situations.

You can ask many types of questions to get an idea of a candidate's behaviors. If you're interviewing for a position that requires a high level of customer service, for example, you would focus on questions related to how the candidate communicated with customers in the past.

Interpersonal skills

Almost any job requires some interpersonal skills. Even if a candidate's technical and knowledge competencies are excellent, a lack in interpersonal skills will make it difficult for this person to interact with managers, coworkers, and clients.

For example, an IT technician must be able to communicate effectively with clients to determine what's wrong with their computer systems. So this person has to ask the right questions and be able to listen actively. A lawyer must be able to communicate with clients to apply the law most effectively.

Once you've determined the required competencies for a given position, you can find out whether the candidates demonstrate those competencies by asking the right questions.

Behavioral-based interview questions should always be job related. They should be designed to elicit examples of how candidates behaved in relevant work situations, what they learned, and whether their experience applies to the given job and work environment.

Question problems

This question doesn't ask candidates to provide any specific information about their ability to work with others in a work context.

It also doesn't focus specifically on what's relevant for the particular job you need to fill. How must a candidate be able to respond to others and in what types of contexts?

A better, behavioral-based question to ask would be "Tell me about a time when you struggled to work with a particular colleague."

This question investigates the candidate's actual behavior in a past, job-related situation and so elicits information that's directly relevant.

Question

Which are two main characteristics of behavioral-based interviewing?

Options:

1. It focuses on determining whether candidates can apply the skills required to perform a given job

2. It involves finding out about candidates' past experiences

3. It involves putting pressure on candidates so you can assess their responses

4. It involves asking candidates personal questions about their lives outside of work

Answer:

Option 1: This option is correct. The purpose of behavioral-based interviewing is to determine whether candidates have required competencies – the skills and abilities to perform a particular job.

Option 2: This is a correct option. Behavioral-based interviewing involves finding out how candidates handled specific situations in the past to determine whether they have the required competencies for the job at hand.

Option 3: This option is incorrect. A behavioral-based interview aims to find out how candidates behave and think, based on how they've handled situations in the past. It doesn't involve pressuring or provoking candidates.

Option 4: This is an incorrect option. In a behavioral-based interview, the questions you ask should relate directly to the competencies required for a particular job.

Minimizing bias

Because behavioral-based interviews focus on facts about a candidate's job-related situations, they tend to minimize bias. They help ensure candidates' responses are relevant and help prevent interviewers from drawing the wrong conclusions.

These are just some of the biases you should be aware of:

- halo bias, in which candidates' strength in one area causes interviewers to view other areas more favorably,
- first impression bias, in which interviewers judge candidates before giving them a fair chance to respond to questions,
- stereotype bias, in which interviewers believe that just because candidates fit into a certain category, they will or won't have the right abilities,
- similarity bias, which occurs when interviewers favor candidates that are similar to themselves, confusing personal similarity with ability,

- contrast bias, in which interviewers' judgments of candidates are based on how well other candidates did in previous interviews, and
- excessive harshness, when interviewers unfairly rate all candidates poorly and disregard their strengths.

Using behavioral-based questions can't completely prevent bias – interviewers need to make a conscious effort to avoid jumping to conclusions about candidates. But these questions do help interviewers move away from stereotyping, gut feelings, and biases. You find out whether candidates can and will do the job, and whether they're a "fit" with the culture and values of the prospective organization.

Question

Which are the main characteristics of behavioral-based interviewing?

Options:

1. It uses candidates' previous behavior to forecast how they'll behave on the job if hired

2. It aims to determine whether candidates have the competencies needed for a particular job

3. It involves asking questions directly related to candidates' job performance

4. It helps prevent subjective judgment by focusing on facts about candidates' behavior in real situations

5. It allows candidates to prepare the right answers to every question you ask

6. It determines how candidates might behave by presenting a hypothetical situation

Answer:

Option 1: This is a correct option. Using behavioral-based questions, you determine how candidates behaved in the past as an indicator of how they're likely to behave in similar situations in the future.

Option 2: This option is correct. The focus in a behavioral-based interview is on determining whether candidates have demonstrated required competencies through their past behavior.

Option 3: This is a correct option. Behavioral-based questions should be designed to test for competencies required for a specific job.

Option 4: This option is correct. Behavioral-based questions minimize bias by focusing on the facts surrounding real situations.

Option 5: This is an incorrect option. Because traditional interview questions are familiar and accessible, they enable candidates to prepare the "right" answers. But these answers may be unrelated to the competencies required for the job.

Option 6: This option is incorrect. Behavioral-based questions focus on candidates' past behaviors, rather than on how they might behave in a given fictitious scenario.

Behavioral-based interviewing involves determining whether candidates have the required competencies for a given job and asking questions about past experience that relates to those competencies. Behavioral-based interviewing also helps minimize bias in the interviewing process.

BEHAVIORAL-BASED QUESTIONS

Behavioral-based questions

Developing behavioral-based questions

When faced with the task of employing the most suitable job candidate from a group of individuals, you want to make sure you make the right choice for your company. It's therefore important that your behavioral-based interviews are effective. To be effective, you need to know two things – what competencies the job requires and how to formulate effective behavioral-based questions for determining whether candidates have these competencies.

The first step in developing effective behavioral-based questions is to identify which specific competencies candidates need to perform the job for which you're interviewing.

You should draw these competencies from the job description, which details the responsibilities and duties associated with the job.

For instance, an interviewer is reviewing the job description for a content editor, who needs to be able to edit and prepare content for online publication.

He identifies the specific competencies required by assessing the tasks and responsibilities that the successful candidate will have to assume.

These include editing content to meet standards for publication on the site and updating and communicating standards to all content producers.

Question

Which competencies do you think an interviewer could derive from the responsibilities associated with the job of content editor?

The responsibilities for the position are listed as "edits content so it meets standards for publication on site" and "updates and communicates standards to content producers."

Options:

1. Creates web-based designs
2. Pays attention to detail
3. Has experience in web content development
4. Communicates well verbally and in writing

Answer:

Option 1: This is an incorrect option. The appointed candidate won't be responsible for the design, so being able to create web-based designs isn't a required competency.

Option 2: This option is correct. The ability to pay attention to detail is a competency required of a content editor. A competency is a behavior or set of behaviors describing the expected performance in a particular work context – in this case, as a content editor, where proofreading skills are key.

Option 3: This option is incorrect. The appointed candidate won't be responsible for developing web content. Also, work experience is a skill or skill set, not a competency.

Option 4: This is a correct option. The candidate appointed to the position must be able to communicate well in order to update and communicate standards to content producers.

Based on the responsibilities associated with the content editor role, an interviewer identifies the required competencies, which include communicating effectively – both verbally and in writing – and paying attention to detail.

Once you know the competencies you need to look for in candidates, you can translate each of these into a relevant behavioral-based question. This type of question asks for a specific example of how a candidate behaved in the past, to test for a required competency. Some typical lead-ins you might use for these questions are "Can you describe..." "Can you give me an example of..." and "Tell me about..."

Now that the interviewer for the copy editor position has identified the competencies required, he needs to develop questions. He starts with the competency "Communicates effectively both verbally and in writing."

The first question he comes up with is "Describe the most difficult or complex idea, situation, or process you have ever had to explain to someone. How did you explain it? Were you successful?"

He also plans to ask "Can you provide an example of what happened when someone misunderstood something you wrote. How did you determine that you had been misunderstood? How did you make yourself clear?"

The interviewer then considers the second competency – "Pays attention to detail."

The first question he develops for this competency is "Give me an example of a time where your attention to detail helped you avoid making a mistake."

He also develops a second question to test this particular competency – "Describe a situation where you didn't pay as close attention to the details as you should have."

Like the questions for the content editor job, behavioral-based questions should have these characteristics:

- they should always test for required competencies – those really needed for someone to perform the given job successfully,
- they should be open-ended questions, requiring more than a "yes" or "no" response, and
- they should be designed to elicit specific examples of past behavior.

See each characteristic to learn more about it.

Test for required competencies

Behavioral-based questions that don't relate to relevant competencies won't provide you with the information you need to fill the position effectively.

For example, you wouldn't investigate how a candidate dealt with managing difficult employees unless the available position involves supervising others. You would, however, want to ask someone applying for a position that requires conflict management skills questions related to this. For example, you might ask "How did you facilitate a creative solution between employees in the past?" or say "Tell me about a time when you didn't properly handle a disagreement with a coworker."

Be open-ended

Open-ended questions are designed to elicit detailed responses, rather than short or single-word answers. To gain insight into candidates' competencies based on their past behavior, you need to encourage them to elaborate.

An example of an open-ended behavioral-based question is "Can you give an example of a conflict situation you encountered and how you dealt with it?" The response to this is likely to yield far more focused information than the answer to a close-ended question like "Have you dealt successfully with conflict situations?" or "Can you imagine yourself working in a position of authority?"

Ask for specific examples

Behavioral-based questions should be designed to elicit details of a specific situation or task, the actions the person took or didn't take in response, and the impact of these actions. A good example might be "Can you give an example of how you followed up with a client who didn't respond to calls or e-mails?"

Candidates sometimes answer even specific questions in broad terms. So you may need to follow your questions up with additional probing questions. For instance, you might say "Go back to the beginning, when you first realized there was a problem. How did you respond to the problem?"

Sometimes – although not always – it can help to include superlative adjectives in behavioral-based questions. These can help candidates focus on specific incidents, so that they can respond with relevant examples.

For example, you might ask a question such as "What's the most frustrating experience you ever had with a client, and how did you react?" or – going back to the content editor position – "What kind of writing do you do best? Give me an example."

When considering the format of questions you'll ask during an interview, make sure you're familiar with the distinction between behavioral and situational interview questions.

Situational questions are based on hypothetical behavior and are used to gain insight into a candidate's anticipated behavior in a hypothetical situation.

For instance, a situational question would be "If an unhappy customer approaches you about a defective product, how would you handle the situation?" A behavioral-based question, regarding the same situation, would be "Tell me about a time you had to deal with an unhappy client. How did you handle the situation?"

Question

A medical receptionist must be competent in verbally communicating appropriately in a diverse range of situations and managing the administration of payments in a busy doctors' practice.

Based on these job requirements, which are the appropriate behavioral-based questions for asking candidates during interviews?

Options:

1. "Can you describe a situation in the past when you had to follow up on a late payment?"

2. "Tell me about a time you had to deal with a patient who was anxious and difficult to calm down. How did you handle the situation?"

3. "Do you think you'd find it difficult to work night shifts if you were to get this job?" 4. "Did you get along well with colleagues in your last job?"

Answer:

Option 1: This option is correct. This question is open-ended, reflective of identified competencies, and gets candidates to provide detailed examples of past behaviors.

Option 2: This is a correct option. This question asks how candidates dealt with a past situation that relates directly to situations a medical receptionist is likely to encounter. The question is also appropriate because it's open-ended and asks for a specific example.

Option 3: This option is incorrect. This isn't a behavioral-based question. It isn't designed to elicit an example of how candidates dealt with a particular situation in the past. It doesn't test for competencies specific to the position of a medical receptionist.

Option 4: This is an incorrect option. This isn't a good behavioral-based question because it's close-ended. A simple answer like "yes" won't provide you with useful information about candidates' competencies. It also isn't specific enough to provide you with the information you need to assess whether a candidate has the required competencies.

You should develop behavioral-based interview questions by first identifying the competencies required for a job. These questions should be open-ended and designed to elicit specific examples of how candidates dealt with situations or tasks in the past.

STRATEGIES FOR ASKING QUESTIONS

Strategies for asking questions

Strategies for complete answers

Even in response to good behavioral-based interview questions, it's rare that candidates will include enough – or the right – information. So to judge their level of competency in handling specific situations, you need to follow up with more questions. For example, you might ask questions that probe for more details about a particular aspect of the candidate's actions or you might ask about how the candidate resolved a situation and what the outcome was.

When you ask behavior-based questions, you want to get an answer that has these three elements:
- a description of a specific, real situation or problem in which the candidate demonstrated a required skill or competency for the position,
- details of actions taken by the candidate to deal with the situation, and
- the results of the actions taken.

Question

An interviewer poses a question to a job candidate: "Tell me about a problem that you encountered with a colleague in your previous job. What steps did you take to deal with it?"

Which of the three example responses is a complete one that doesn't require further investigation?

Options:

1. "There was one colleague I never saw eye-to-eye with. We just had completely different ways of handling situations."
2. "A colleague and I had differing ideas about a client's needs. We decided to go to our supervisor, and got a fresh perspective on the client's needs."
3. "A former colleague and I found it difficult to work together because our personalities clashed."

Answer:

The incorrect responses are not specific enough about the problems encountered and don't mention what steps were taken to find resolution. The correct response details what the problem was and what steps were taken to resolve it.

Four strategies can help ensure you get complete answers to behavioral-based questions:

1. at the start of an interview, ask a broad, open question about an example of the candidate's past behavior
2. ask a more specific question about the candidate's role in the situation described
3. ask questions about any actions the candidate took to resolve the situation, and
4. ask about the results of the candidate's actions

Ask a broad, open question

If you start by asking candidates broad, open, behavioral-based questions, you give them enough scope to pick whatever example they feel is most appropriate. This helps get candidates speaking about their experiences, beyond what's in their resumes. It lays the foundation for successive questions, which you can use to obtain more specific information.

Peggy is the managing director of an events management company. She's interviewing Catherine for the position of events coordinator. Follow along as Peggy asks Catherine a broad, behavioral-based question.

Peggy: Catherine, can you tell me about an event you organized that was difficult or challenging?

Catherine: I planned a large charity event in which several local celebrities participated. It was really tricky to coordinate. We had to respond to lots of last-minute changes and we had to factor in the need for tight security.

The event Catherine describes in response to the broad, open question that Peggy asks at the start will lead to several more specific questions about Catherine's particular role in the event. Peggy needs to find out as much as she can about Catherine's past behavior as it relates to the competencies required for the job. Catherine will need to prove she can provide a high level of client satisfaction, organize diverse aspects of an event, and handle public relations issues for events.

When candidates describe a particular situation – like the charity event that Catherine mentioned – it's important that you establish when it occurred.

This tells you how recently candidates put their skills into practice.

And remember that you can ask candidates for a more recent example if you feel the one they've provided happened too long ago.

Question

Which question is a good one for opening a behavioral-based interview with a candidate?

Options:

1. "Tell me about a time when you had to adapt to changes in company policy. How did you do this?"

2. "You mentioned that you've been in a management position before. When was this and for how long did you hold this position?"

3. "In your former position as team leader, how many staff members reported directly to you?"

Answer:

Questions that are not behavioral based ask the candidate to provide specific information. A behavioral-based question allows the candidate to answer by recalling a past situation and how it was dealt with. The response often prompts follow-up questions.

Sometimes, a candidate may not be able to think of an example. In such cases, you shouldn't just move on to the next question. Nervousness may be hindering the candidate from recalling a relevant example.

If this happens, tell the candidate it's fine to spend some time thinking about an example and give the person a bit of time for reflection.

Or you can ask the question in a different way or ask a completely different question about the same skill area.

Ask a specific question

Once a candidate has responded to a broad behavioral-based question by recalling a particular situation, it's time to ask a more specific question about the candidate's role in that situation.

Peggy's interview with Catherine for the position of events coordinator progresses. Follow along as Peggy asks Catherine more specific questions about the challenging event she recently organized to find out if her experience matches the competencies for the job.

Peggy: It sounds like a big event, and I can imagine it was challenging. How long ago was it held?

Catherine: It was three months ago. It's the most recent major event I've organized.

Peggy: And what exactly was your role – what were your particular responsibilities?

Catherine: We had to secure a venue, publicize the event, organize sponsors, and arrange catering.

Peggy: That covers a lot. Were you in charge of all those areas?

Catherine: Yes. I negotiated the contract for the venue and created the marketing packet. I also met with potential sponsors. I arranged the catering, which ended up being more problematic than I anticipated.

Often candidates use the plural form in their answers. For instance, they may use phrases like "We thought that..." or "Our team decided that..." In the previous example, Catherine describes her responsibilities using "we." When this happens, you should probe to get candidates talking about their roles, using "I" language. It's important candidates separate their role from that of others so you can find out more about their responsibilities and actions.

By following up on her initial broad, open question, Peggy gets useful information regarding Catherine's role in coordinating the charity event.

This helps Peggy find out more about how well Catherine's past behavior matches to the competencies for an event coordinator in Peggy's company.

Peggy may want to ask further questions about the catering problems Catherine hints at. Catherine's response may reveal how well she matches to another competency for the job, which is to quickly solve problems that may arise during the planning or running of an event.

Question

In an interview for which a key competency is the ability to make quick and effective decisions, you ask a candidate for an example of a time when she had to make a quick decision. Her response is "We had to respond quickly when a major supplier went bankrupt, but there was no time left to find a new one. So our team completely redesigned the product."

You now need to find out more about the candidate's behavior.

How should you proceed?

Options:

1. Ask the candidate what her specific role was when the decision was made.

2. Ask the candidate to provide a further example of a time when her team made a quick decision.

3. Ask what the final result of the decisions was. For example, was the product a success?

4. Ask the candidate another broad question relating to a different competency.

Answer:

You should ask a specific question about what her role was when the decision was made to redesign the product. Until you do this, you won't know if she, or someone else in her team, made the decision that resolved the problem.

Ask questions about actions

Once candidates have told you about a particular situation and their role in it, you have to find out more about the actions they took in that situation.

Candidates normally choose to talk about situations that were successful. But you need to find out the extent to which the candidate was responsible for the success – was it because of other factors, like the hard work of other team members or luck, for example?

This step is one of the most important – it can prevent you from assuming the candidate has competencies this person doesn't really have.

What do you do if candidates talk in overly broad terms about the actions they took? In such cases, you need to ask probing questions to get more information.

For instance, you could follow up a reply with a question like "That's a fairly broad answer. How exactly did you overcome those obstacles?"

But note that your response doesn't have to be posed as a question. It could also be a statement, such as "Tell me exactly what steps you took."

A useful technique is to paraphrase what a candidate has said and then follow up with a question. Many follow-up questions relate specifically to what the candidate has said. This makes it hard to prepare a totally comprehensive list of probing questions before an interview. But to become a skilled interviewer, you need to learn to think on your feet to come up with additional, relevant questions to ask about candidates' actions.

It may not always be enough to know how candidates behaved in particular situations. In some cases, you may also need to understand why candidates acted in the way they did. Remember, a candidate could demonstrate a right behavior by chance rather than through careful thought and insight into a situation. So occasionally you should try to ask "why" questions – for example, "Why did you decide on that solution?"

In some situations, you'll want to get negative – or "failed" – examples from a candidate. These can sometimes be of a value equal to or greater than a positive incident the candidate could relate.

For example, you might ask "Can you tell me about an occasion when you didn't meet a customer's needs?"

This type of question may be particularly useful for a competency of maintaining customer relationships effectively.

As the interview continues, Peggy finds out that the caterers pulled out three weeks before the event. Follow along as Peggy now tries to find out more about how Catherine dealt with the situation.

Peggy: I imagine that could be disastrous. How did you deal with it?

Catherine: I found a solution, thankfully, and the event was a success.

Peggy: You say you found a solution. What exactly was your solution? What did you do?

Catherine: I phoned around and met with other caterers to discuss what I needed. Luckily I found one who actually ended up providing a better menu at the same price as my original caterer.

Question

A job applicant for a managerial position has answered some questions related to the competency "plans projects effectively." He has described his role in planning a complex project, including some of the problems he encountered. In particular, he mentions it was difficult planning the timing and sequencing of activities because many of the resources were unavailable when needed.

Which are appropriate ways to proceed with the interview?

Options:

1. Tell the candidate you're impressed he had to deal with so much and ask a broad question related to another competency

2. Ask the candidate for a further example of when he dealt with an uncomfortable task

3. Ask the candidate how he dealt with the situation and why he chose to deal with it in that way

4. Repeat what the candidate has said in your own words and follow this up with a probing question

Answer:

It's important to find out how the candidate dealt with the situation – what actions he took. You may also ask why he chose the solution he did, in order to understand his thought processes. This will give you insight into his competencies, as well as his reasoning. You may also want to repeat what the candidate said in your own words and follow this up with a probing question.

Ask about results

The final strategy for getting a complete answer to a behavioral-based question is to ask about the results a candidate achieved. What was the outcome of the actions this person took in the given situation? This provides you with the end of the story, so to speak, and allows the candidate to summarize what the achievements were in the given situation.

It's important to question the results candidates claim to have achieved, especially if they use vague terms that include comparators such as "fewer" or "better." Prompt them to quantify what they're saying. For example, you could ask "How exactly was the process better?" or "What do you mean by fewer?"

You may also want to ask candidates what lessons they've learned from the situations or experiences they've described.

In her interview with Catherine, Peggy continues to ask specific questions. Follow along as Peggy asks about the results of Catherine's actions.

Peggy: You said the event was one of your best. How so?

Catherine: The feedback I received from the client and from those who attended was all positive. And the client hired us again to manage another event and recommended us to some of his contacts.

Peggy: So would you describe the results you achieve in most of your events as very successful – like this one – or moderately successful?

Catherine: I've planned quite a few successful events.

Peggy: You say "quite a few." Could you be more specific in telling me how many?

Catherine: Since entering the field two years ago, I've coordinated 16 successful events.

Peggy: What did you learn from your experience coordinating the charity event?

Catherine: One thing's for sure – always have a backup plan.

Remember, when using behavioral-based questions during an interview, it's important to avoid leading or loaded questions.

For example, Peggy asks Catherine a loaded question – "So would you describe the results you achieve in most of your events as very successful – like this one – or moderately successful"? Such a question can inhibit applicants from providing their own, more accurate responses.

Meanwhile, leading questions imply that there's only one correct answer. They make it obvious what the interviewer wants or expects to hear in response.

Question

In response to your question, a job applicant describes the actions she took to deal with a rude client.

Which are good ways to proceed with the interview?

Options:

1. Ask her about the results of her actions in dealing with the customer

2. Ask her what, if anything, she learned from the experience

3. Tell the applicant what you would have done in her situation

4. Ask the applicant if she learned patience or negotiating skills from the experience

Answer:

Option 1: This option is correct. After the candidate explains what actions she took, you should question what the results of those actions were.

Option 2: This is a correct option. You can ask the candidate about what she learned from the situation in which she had to use her skills.

Option 3: This is an incorrect option. Once the candidate tells you how she dealt with the situation, you should ask what the results of her actions were and what she learned from the experience.

Option 4: This option is incorrect. This is a loaded question that forces the candidate to choose between two answers. You should get the candidate to tell you what she learned rather than giving her a limited set of options to choose from.

Four main strategies can help you elicit complete answers to behavioral-based interview questions.

First use a broad, open question to ask a candidate for a specific example of past behavior that relates to a required competency. Follow this with one or more specific questions about the applicant's role in the situation described. Then ask about the actions the applicant took. Finally, find out what the results of those actions were.

CHAPTER V - SELECTING THE RIGHT CANDIDATE

CHAPTER V - Selecting the Right Candidate

Once the chosen candidate accepts a position, you might think the hiring process is over. But an important step remains – you need to inform all unsuccessful candidates of your decision. Failing to do this can reflect badly on your company.

In this chapter, you'll learn how to evaluate candidates once you've completed interviews, how to check their references effectively, and how best to make an offer to the candidate you select. This will equip you to secure the best possible candidate for a job.

EVALUATING A CANDIDATE AFTER AN INTERVIEW

Evaluating a candidate after an interview

Structure your approach

Interviews, testing, and checking references are ways for interviewers to collect relevant information about a candidate. However, collecting information is only part of the process. To hire the right candidate for the job, you have to be able to evaluate the candidate by using that information effectively.

Interviewers often expend a lot of energy on the structure of the interview – for example, by deciding what questions to ask candidates and how to ask them. This is because interviews are a key method of getting relevant information from candidates.

What's sometimes overlooked is that it's just as important to structure the evaluation process, based on the information you've obtained.

Question

Which approach do you think is best for making a decision about whether a candidate is suitable for a position?

Options:

1. Decide during the interview, based on what the candidate says and your gut instincts

2. Make a judgment early on in the interview and use this to make a decision after it's finished

3. Wait until after the interview to make any decision, once you've reviewed and analyzed your notes about the candidate.

Answer:

Option 1: This option is incorrect. While it's fairly common for interviewers to use this approach, it can lead to bad hiring decisions. During an interview, it's not possible to assess all the information at your disposal about a candidate, and you're likely to be subject to bias.

Option 2: This option is incorrect. It can be hard to put initial judgments aside, which in turn means you won't be able to evaluate all the information about candidates objectively. So it's best not to form these judgments until after interviews, once you've used a structured, objective process to assess all candidates.

Option 3: This is the correct option. It's best to form a decision only after interviews are complete and after you've used a structured approach to evaluate all candidates based on an objective set of job-related criteria.

To help you make an effective hiring decision, you can structure your approach to evaluating candidates using three steps. Detail and review the candidate's behaviors, compare these behaviors to job expectations, and finally rate each candidate.

So to conduct a structured evaluation of candidates you've interviewed, you first need to detail and review the information you've collected. This process should start during interviews, when you take notes about candidates' responses.

During an interview, the notes you take should consist just of keywords and short phrases. These will act as reminders of what a candidate has said, but they don't require that you spend too long writing and not enough time listening.

Immediately after the interview, you should expand your notes to include relevant details, while you still remember their intent and so you don't miss anything important.

When you're taking and expanding on your notes, you should follow three main guidelines: avoid subjective language, which reflects opinion rather than fact

don't record opinions without job-related facts to back them up, and refer to job-related facts

See each guideline to learn more about it.

Avoid subjective language

You should avoid subjective language because it can indicate that you're basing a hiring decision on criteria that are unfair and inappropriate. Instead, take time after an interview to expand your notes and make sure they're objective.

An example of a subjective note is "The candidate is talkative." To rephrase this objectively, you could record something like "The job requires good verbal skills. The candidate was clear and concise throughout the interview." In this way, you successfully compare the candidate's behavior against a clear job requirement.

Don't record opinions

When you're writing notes in an interview, you should avoid adding personal opinions. Everything you record should relate to the candidate's ability to meet the job requirements. To do this, you should back up your thoughts or opinions with job-related information.

So instead of saying "I feel that the candidate isn't what we're searching for," you should note something along the lines of "Because of the candidate's lack of experience in managing a diverse team, he isn't a suitable candidate for this position." Here the interviewer is backing up the statement by saying why he's reached a specific conclusion.

Refer to job-related facts

As soon as you've finished interviewing, you need to record the details about whether the candidate has demonstrated the ability to meet each of the key requirements for the job.

You quote a candidate to back up an observation you record. For example, if you get the feeling a candidate has a negative attitude toward some aspects of the job, you might record that the candidate said "I'll work overtime, but I need sufficient advance notice."

Then, when it's time to write up this interview, you can state "This job calls for extensive overtime with little advance notice. When asked how she felt about this, the candidate replied 'I'll work overtime, but I need sufficient advance notice.' " This indicates that the candidate finds one of the job requirements objectionable.

When you properly document what you've learned about a candidate during an interview, you ensure you'll be able to evaluate the candidate objectively. Also, you'll be able to justify your eventual hiring decision. Your notes will make it clear that you had objective reasons for deciding that a candidate either did or didn't meet the job requirements.

Question

How can Adam effectively detail and review Sandy's behaviors after he's interviewed her for a marketing manager position?

The first question Adam asks is "What problems did you encounter in your previous position?" and the notes for this are "Time deadlines, workload." The second question is "How did you tackle it?" and the notes for this are "Delayed deadlines, more employees." The last question is "Did you have to do a lot of over time?" and the note for this is "Wrong attitude."

Options:

1. Note that "Sandy struggled with deadlines due to heavy work load."

2. Revise his notes to make them objective.

3. Explain "wrong attitude" with Sandy's quote "I like stability. It ensures consistent output." 4. Expand his notes with personal opinions.

5. Ask a colleague to review his initial notes for red flags that rule out candidates.

Answer:

Option 1: This is a correct option. After the interview, Adam should expand on his notes to avoid forgetting important information.

Option 2: This option is correct. Adam should revise his notes so he doesn't make unfair judgements. His notes should always relate to job requirements.

Option 3: This is a correct option. Instead of writing "wrong attitude," Adam should relate Sandy's quote to a job requirement, such as flexibility during times of change.

Option 4: This option is incorrect. Adam should avoid personal opinions when expanding his notes. He should stick to job-related facts.

Option 5: This is an incorrect option. Adam's colleague may not understand his initial notes. He needs to expand on them objectively and relate them to job requirements.

Compare to job requirements

Once you've detailed and reviewed what you've learned about each candidate, you need to compare this information more thoroughly against job requirements. Your purpose is to determine whether the candidates' behaviors show they have the required competencies to do the job.

During this process, you should check each candidate's information against the required competencies for the job.

For example, during an interview for the position of call center team lead, an interviewer would want to discover that the successful candidate is able to manage difficult or irate customers.

The interviewer's notes remind him of a candidate who outlined a past situation in which she did just the right things to handle a difficult customer. By the end of the call, the customer was satisfied with the service. In this case, the interviewer could put a checkmark next to this competency before moving on to the next.

The interviewer's notes remind him of a candidate who outlined a past situation in which she did just the right things to handle a difficult customer. By the end of the call, the customer was satisfied with the service. In this case, the interviewer could put a checkmark next to this competency before moving on to the next.

Jessica's answer

Jessica describes a time she worked on a project with very tight deadlines. She explains it was important to meet the deadlines because the client was a particularly important one. She couldn't let the situation get to her and she had to keep focused. Jessica says her way of dealing with stress is to jot down a list of everything that needs to be done and then to prioritize what's on the list. Jessica says this helps her manage stress and prevents her from wasting time on unnecessary tasks.

Latitia's answer

Latitia tells Martin that she felt very stressed in her previous position and she gets flustered when she's stressed. However, she says she always feels better after a good night's rest.

Jessica's response includes the components of Martin's preferred answer and she doesn't demonstrate any unacceptable behaviors. Latitia's answer, on the other hand, effectively demonstrated only one of the components.

Martin now has a straightforward and objective way to evaluate the two candidates. Based on their responses, it's clear that Jessica is better equipped than Latitia in terms of the ability to handle stress.

You can use an evaluation form to help you evaluate candidates fairly, linking information about them to required competencies. A form such as this can help you clarify differences between candidates objectively.

Question

Bonnie interviews Neil for an IT technician position. After the interview, she needs to compare Neil's behaviors against the job expectations.

How can she do this effectively?

Options:

1. Link Neil's description of working well in a diverse workplace to the job requirement of working across departments

2. Note that Neil's unwillingness to work overtime is unacceptable because the job requires it

3. Compare Neil's answer about how he developed evaluation techniques with her preferred response, which is that he demonstrates initiative

4. Use a structured form that lists the job requirements to check off the requirements that Neil demonstrates

5. Note Neil's unprofessional first impression

6. Compare Neil's competency in meeting deadlines with her own to find out if he's suitable

Answer:

Option 1: This option is correct. Bonnie should focus on matching Neil's responses to specific job requirements to determine whether he has the required competencies for the job. In this case, Neil's response matches with one of the job requirements.

Option 2: This is a correct option. As well as matching Neil's responses against job requirements, Bonnie should check for any responses indicating unacceptable behaviors. These could disqualify him from further consideration.

Option 3: This option is correct. Bonnie can determine whether Neil's responses match her preferred responses.

In this case, Neil's answer matches with Bonnie's preferred response.

Option 4: This is a correct option. Using a structured form to evaluate all candidates will make it easier for Bonnie to asses Neil's suitability for the job, remain objective, and compare different candidates.

Option 5: This option is incorrect. An interviewer shouldn't consider first impressions, which are often not objective. Bonnie should discount these and evaluate Neil by comparing his behaviors with the job requirements.

Option 6: This is an incorrect option. If Bonnie is searching for candidates that behave like her, she's showing bias. Instead, she needs to focus on whether Neil's responses to interview questions demonstrate the required competencies for the job.

Rate candidates

Once you've determined how well each candidate meets job requirements, you can rate the candidates using a scale you devise. You can rate candidates' responses or behaviors by giving them each a numerical score, based on how well they match to a particular job requirement or preferred answer.

For example, you might allocate minus one point for each unacceptable part of an answer and plus one point for each preferred part of an answer.

So Latitia's answer to Martin's question about handling stress scores a total of minus one because her responses meet only one of the three requirements in Martin's preferred responses.

Some organizations score zero for an unacceptable answer – essentially ignoring it and concentrating on the positive scores for standard answers. Both approaches are acceptable, provided you're consistent about which you use.

It's likely that some competencies you've identified as required are more important than others. To reflect this, you can choose to use a weighted scale to rate candidates' responses.

To do this, you assign a score to the candidate's response to each question. You then assign a criticality factor to each of these questions, based on the relative importance of the competency it's designed to test for.

Lastly, you multiply each score by the corresponding criticality value to get a final score for each question.

Once you've rated a candidate's answers, you add all the scores to get a total score. You do the same for all the remaining candidates, so you can compare the total scores for each candidate. This method helps you make a final decision – especially if you've been left with two or three strong candidates and need to clarify the differences in their suitability.

Question

David wants to employ a new accountant. He's interviewed Margaret and has collected and analyzed information about her responses to his interview questions. Now he needs to rate Margaret.

How can David rate Margaret effectively in relation to job expectations?

Options:

1. Score Margaret's answer of how she becomes flustered under stress with a negative point, as it doesn't match the job requirement

2. Give Margaret's mathematical competency a higher score in a weighted rating system because it's critical

3. Assign Margaret's response a score out of three for the required competency of interpersonal skills 4. Sum up all positive and negative points to get a total and then compare this with other candidates 5. Score Margaret according to her similarity to the previous person who held the position

6. Use his first impression to assign Margaret's professionalism a score of between 1 and 10

Answer:

Option 1: This option is correct. David rates Margaret by deducting points for unacceptable responses and adding points for those that indicate the required competencies. Margaret's response is unacceptable and therefore David deducts points from her score.

Option 2: This is a correct option. David multiplies Margaret's score for each question by a criticality factor, based on the relative importance of the competencies the questions are designed to test for. In this case, David weights the mathematical competency highly because it's a critical factor for an accounting position.

Option 3: This option is correct. To rate Margaret objectively, David assigns scores to her responses based on the extent to which she shows she has the required competencies.

Option 4: This is a correct option. David adds Margaret's scores for all questions to calculate a total score. He'll then compare this score to the final scores for other candidates to determine who best meets job requirements.

Option 5: This option is incorrect. David should score Margaret based only on whether she has the required competencies for the job. Comparing similarities in people can lead to biased decisions.

Option 6: This is an incorrect option. Judging Margaret based on his general impressions – instead of in relation to clear job requirements – can lead to David making bad hiring decisions.

Question

Drawing on what you've learned about evaluating candidates, what do you think are the benefits of being able to do this effectively?

Options:

1. You'll be better able to clarify the differences between candidates objectively
2. You'll be able to justify your hiring decisions
3. You'll be able to back up your personal impressions of who's most suitable for a position
4. You'll be able to eliminate the need to train the candidates who are hired

Answer:

The benefits of evaluating a candidate effectively are that you can decipher the differences between candidates and justify your decisions.

Option 1: This option is correct. When you have two or more strong candidates who might be suitable for a position, evaluating them using a structured process and a rating system will help you make an objective decision. This means you're more likely to make a good selection.

Option 2: This is a correct option. If you use a structured evaluation technique that's consistent for every candidate, you'll be able to justify your hiring decisions – you can show you've conducted a fair evaluation process.

Option 3: This option is incorrect. An interviewer shouldn't include personal opinions in the evaluation process. This incorporates bias, which can result in poor hiring decisions.

Option 4: This is an incorrect option. Even if you conduct an effective evaluation and hire a suitable candidate, it's possible this person will require specific training.

You can structure the process of evaluating candidates you've interviewed by following three steps – detail and review each candidate's behaviors, compare the behaviors against job expectations, and then rate all the candidates using an appropriate scoring system.

HOW TO CHECK REFERENCES OF CANDIDATES

How to check references of candidates

Checking references

It makes good sense to check the references of a prospective employee. Reference checks aim to find out about a candidate's past behavior and performance from people who have first-hand experience – such as past managers, colleagues, or clients. As the interviewer, you'll be the best person to speak to them because you've become familiar with the candidate.

As important as reference checks are, however, not all organizations contact their potential employees' references. It may be that they don't know whether doing this is legitimate, they don't have the time, or they don't think they'll find out anything important. But they're wrong on all counts – references are necessary. They provide useful information that'll help you decide whether a candidate is right for the job.

Reference checks have several purposes when done properly:
- they validate or disprove facts you gathered from the interview itself,
- they clarify or add other, valuable data to the decision-making process, and
- they bring new facts about the candidate's personality or past behavior to light.

It makes good sense to check the references of a prospective employee. Reference checks aim to find out about a candidate's past behavior and performance from people who have first-hand experience – such as past managers, colleagues, or clients. As the interviewer, you'll be the best person to speak to them because you've become familiar with the candidate.

As important as reference checks are, however, not all organizations contact their potential employees' references. It may be that they don't know whether doing this is legitimate, they don't have the time, or they don't think they'll find out anything important. But they're wrong on all counts – references are necessary. They provide useful information that'll help you decide whether a candidate is right for the job.

Reference checks have several purposes when done properly:
- they validate or disprove facts you gathered from the interview itself,
- they clarify or add other, valuable data to the decision-making process, and
- they bring new facts about the candidate's personality or past behavior to light.

You can check applicants' references effectively by following three guidelines. First make sure you get references from the candidate, as well as the permission to do reference checks. Then make the call to those references. And finally, ensure you ask them the right sorts of questions.

Getting permission

Whether before or during an interview, you should make sure you get reference information from the candidate. You can let the candidate know in advance that you'll require this information.

Sometimes informing candidates that you're going to check their references can help ensure the answers they give you during interviews are truthful.

You should always get written and signed permission from the candidate before you attempt to check references. Having this permission reassures previous employers that they're authorized to give you information about the candidate. This will release them from any liability.

To get the most out of your reference checks, you should get the contact details of the candidate's supervisors or managers, and not the HR personnel at that person's previous employment. In addition, be sure to contact only those people the candidate has worked with in the previous three years.

Question

Why do you think it's best to get the details of managers and supervisors instead of HR personnel?

Options:

1. Because they can verify specific facts about the applicant's past work

2. Because they'll be able to focus on information from official records

3. Because they won't know the applicant as well as HR personnel and therefore can be more objective

Answer:

Managers and supervisors will be able to give you details and specific examples of job-related skills and competencies. HR personnel often won't know the candidate personally, so the call won't be as informative.

The best person to speak to is the candidate's previous supervisor. The best information is verification of specific facts about the candidate's past work, and a supervisor is in a position to provide this. Check out claims made by the candidate that are related to vital requirements for the new job.

Whenever possible, avoid being transferred to an HR Department. HR personnel may not know the candidate personally. They will give you information taken from records. Someone who knows the candidate will give you a better sense of what this person was like to work with.

It can help to ask the candidate to get in touch with former supervisors so they know you're going to call.

You can also make it a condition of employment to provide reference information to ensure you get the applicant's permission.

Question

What should you do before you check an applicant's references?

Options:

1. Ask the candidate to supply a list of references that you can contact
2. Make sure you get a reference who was the applicant's supervisor at a recent position
3. Get written permission to contact references from the candidate
4. Ask for references from previous employers of ten or more years ago
5. Get references from HR personnel at the applicant's previous organizations

Answer:

Option 1: This is a correct option. You can ask candidates in advance for their reference information or even make it a requirement to provide this information.

Option 2: This option is correct. The best references are supervisors rather than HR personnel – especially supervisors from recent positions.

Option 3: This is a correct option. Former employers will be more willing to talk to you if they know the applicant has given permission for them to do so.

Option 4: This option is incorrect. Typically, you should contact people with whom the candidate has worked in the last three years, at most.

Option 5: This is an incorrect option. HR personnel are less likely to know the candidate personally or be willing to give you information about the candidate.

Making the call

Contacting telephone references is an effective way to gather information about a candidate who you're considering for a job.

Question

Why do you think telephone references are more effective than written ones?

Options:

1. They allow you to assess a former employer's tone of voice

2. They take more time to conduct but are more focused

3. They allow you to ask for clarification of points you don't understand

4. They focus on verifying facts about the candidate, as recorded in HR files

Answer:

Contacting a telephone reference enables you to assess an employer's tone of voice. The tone may indicate which areas you need to explore in more depth. But remember that tone is often a matter of perception. Telephone references provide you with on-the-spot information and you can clarify any points you don't understand. Written references are often laborious and anonymous because the request may be relayed to HR personnel who provide only basic facts from an employee's official file.

It's a good idea to check at least two or three previous employers in case one employer has a positive or negative bias. Checking a number of references also helps you uncover patterns in a candidate's behavior.

Conducting a reference check is much like carrying out an interview. Similar skills are needed – including active listening and encouraging the other person to talk.

And as with interviewing, it's also important to prepare. You should determine what information you need to ask for or verify. Ideally, you should outline this in a reference check form, which you can keep in front of you when you make the call.

How you make the call is also important. To get the most out of it, you should introduce yourself and state your purpose clearly, be friendly but persistent, and know how to win over reluctant references. In this way, you're more likely to get the person talking about the candidate.

See each technique you might use when making a call to a reference to find out more about it.

Introduce yourself

You should begin by introducing yourself and your organization. Then immediately explain that the candidate is applying for a position at your organization and that you'd like to do a reference check. You might say something like "Good afternoon. My name is Liz and I'm a senior manager at Callinsure. A former employee of yours, Scott Anderson, has given you as a reference and I'd like to do a check on him."

It can help to build a bit of rapport with the person as well. If you rush into a reference check in a perfunctory way, it may hinder you from getting the information you need.

Be friendly but persistent

You should ask whether it's a convenient time to do a reference check. It's important to be polite because you're asking the reference to do you a favor by speaking to you.

Some organizations might not allow for reference checking. At the very least, you could verify that the candidate worked for the organization. If the reference won't talk at all, you could also ask that person to recommend someone else within the organization who would be willing to tell you about the candidate.

Win over reluctant references

If the reference is busy or reluctant to talk to you, you can provide your phone number and ask that person to call you back. For example, this can give the reference a chance to verify your identity or to phone the candidate to verify you have permission to do a reference check. In addition, you should mention that anything said during the call will be kept in the strictest confidence. This may help put the reference at ease.

You can also appeal to the reference's common sense. If necessary, you could even refer to legislation that protects employers from litigation.

Once the reference has agreed to speak with you, you may need to give your contact time to find old files or records about the candidate in order to answer your questions.

You should also describe the position the candidate is applying for and what sort of behavior or work habits are required.

Emily has interviewed a promising candidate, Gerald Franks, for an internship at the company she works for, Earth Farm. Gerald seems almost too good to be true, so she'd like to check one of his references. She calls Myra, who was his supervisor in his previous position. Follow along as Emily conducts the call to Myra.

Myra: Hello, Myra speaking.

Emily: Good afternoon. My name is Emily Olsen, and I'm a project manager at Earth Farm. I'm doing a reference check on Gerald Franks, who has applied for a position with our organization. Is this a good time?

Myra: I'm not busy at the moment, but I'm not really sure I can discuss Gerald with you.

Emily: Anything you tell me will be kept strictly confidential.

Myra: I don't know...

Emily: I really won't take up much of your time, but I don't want to hire someone without an idea what his past employers think about him. If you like, I can leave my number with you so you can verify that my organization is legitimate.

Myra: No, that's OK. Would you mind hanging on for a minute while I go find Gerald's file?

Emily: Not at all.

Emily introduces herself politely and tells Myra what she's calling about. She successfully persuades Myra to talk to her, although Myra's reluctant at first. Finally, she gives Myra time to collect the information she needs about the candidate.

Question

Which are effective ways to get a reference talking once you've got this person on the phone?

Options:

1. Mention that the information you receive will be kept confidential

2. Introduce yourself and state your purpose clearly

3. Allow the reference time to verify that you're legitimate

4. If the reference doesn't want to talk to you, back off immediately

5. Don't tell the reference what the new position entails

Answer:

Option 1: This option is correct. If you reassure references that anything they tell you will be kept confidential, they'll feel more comfortable talking to you.

Option 2: This is a correct option. The first thing you need to do is introduce yourself and state your purpose clearly. Then ask whether the person has time to speak to you. This ensures that you're courteous and to the point – traits that people appreciate.

Option 3: This option is correct. If references feel uncomfortable talking to you, you can allow them time to verify that you or your organization is legitimate.

Option 4: This is an incorrect option. While you should remain polite, you should be persistent. As a last resort, you can ask to talk to someone else at the organization instead.

Option 5: This option is incorrect. You should tell the reference what sort of tasks the new position will entail and what work behaviors you're looking for.

To get the most effective information from a reference, you need to ask the right questions. For example, you might start by asking for documented information, such as the period for which a candidate you've interviewed worked for the reference or that person's primary responsibilities.

The person you're talking to may feel more comfortable answering questions about neutral, factual topics at the start of the reference check.

These types of opening questions also help references bring the candidate to mind. Then they'll be better able to answer more open-ended, competency-based questions later on in the conversation.

When you're asking questions during a reference check, it's also important to avoid introducing bias into your questions, to be brief but still thorough, and to focus on job-related questions.

See each guideline for asking the right questions for more details about it.

Avoid bias

You should ask questions in a nonbiased way. For example, rather than asking "Did Joshua have a problem meeting deadlines?" ask "How did Joshua handle meeting deadlines?"

Not only is the first question leading, but it's close ended and therefore may not encourage the reference to elaborate.

Be brief but thorough

You should remember you're asking references to take time out of their day to speak to you. So keep your questions brief and to the point.

But don't rush through them – you also want to get as much information as possible about the candidate. It helps to have a list of questions in front of you so you can move through the reference check quickly but thoroughly.

Focus on job-related questions

You should be sure to ask questions that are job-related and avoid personal questions about the candidate. As when you're interviewing, you should examine the requirements of the position to be filled and build your questions around this information.

For example, some job-related questions for a manager position might be "How would you describe the candidate's management and leadership style?" and "How did the candidate motivate his employees?"

If the reference starts giving you information that's not job-related, it's up to you to steer the conversation back on track.

You should be tactful, however. Don't interrupt references while they're answering your questions, but try to keep the conversation focused.

Some references might – deliberately or not – give you information that's vague or ambiguous. For example, the statement "Joshua gave every impression of being a hard worker" could be interpreted in different ways.

You should probe the reference for clarity, rather than trying to interpret the statement later. For instance, you might ask "Can you give me a specific example?"

After the call, you should thank the reference for giving up valuable time to talk to you. Remember that the reference was under no obligation to talk to you at all.

Follow along as Emily continues her reference check on a candidate who's seeking an internship at the company she works for, Earth Farm.

Emily: Can you verify that Gerald worked for you from March to December last year? And that he left for health reasons?

Myra: Yes, that's right.

Emily: What was his job title and what were his responsibilities?

Myra: He worked as a research assistant, so his main tasks were to collect and summarize articles and to write reports for his team leader.

Emily: He indicated he was in charge of a small group of employees. Is that correct?

Myra: Well, he was part of a team, certainly, and I sometimes asked him to conduct training for new members of the team.

Emily: Thank you. Could you describe his teamwork abilities?

Myra: He was like anyone else, really. He got the job done and interacted with the others to the best of his ability.

Emily: So you're saying he was a good team player?

Myra: Not exactly...I think he's a bit of a loner. He doesn't have a natural predisposition to team work, although he was diligent.

Emily starts off with some close-ended factual questions about the period the candidate worked and his reason for leaving.

She moves on to more open-ended questions about his work processes and responsibilities.

She makes sure she probes Myra's more ambiguous statements, and receives some valuable information as a result.

Question

Which are effective ways to ask questions during a reference check?

Options:

1. Be concise but cover everything you need to
2. Avoid discussions about the candidate's personal life
3. Clarify vague or ambiguous statements
4. Interrupt references firmly if they start going off the topic 5. Don't push the reference for more details

Answer:

Option 1: This option is correct. You should be brief so as not to waste the reference's time, but don't rush through the reference check – get the information you need.

Option 2: This is a correct option. You should keep the discussion focused on job-related issues rather than personal topics.

Option 3: This option is correct. You should make sure you don't misinterpret anything the reference says by clarifying those statements that are vague or ambiguous.

Option 4: This is an incorrect option. You shouldn't interrupt references while they speak, but tactfully steer the conversation in the right direction if it goes off track.

Option 5: This option is incorrect. You should clarify what the reference says if it's ambiguous or vague by asking for more details or examples.

Checking a candidate's references can provide you with important information about the candidate's suitability, and enable you to verify facts and impressions you gleaned from an interview.

To check references effectively, you first need to get at least two references from the candidate and written permission to contact them. Phoning references is preferable to contacting them in writing and calls should be concise, friendly, and thorough. It's important to keep the conversation focused on job-related topics by asking the right questions in the right way.

MAKING AN OFFER TO A CANDIDATE

Making an offer to a candidate

Final decision

You've completed the interviewing process, evaluated all the candidates, checked references, and identified the best person for the job. Now you need to make an offer. But this isn't as simple as saying "I pick you." What if the candidate says "no" to the offer?

It's important to be persuasive about why the person should work for your company.

So before actually making an offer, you need to consider factors like the candidate's possible requirements in terms of life balance, compensation, and a challenging work environment.

You should also consider the candidate's goals and how well you can accommodate these in the offer you're willing to make.

It can help to follow three strategies when making your offer:

1. determine an offer that's competitive,

2. make the offer both verbally and in writing, and
3. inform the other candidates who have not been selected.

Determine the offer

As the first step, you need to determine a job offer that's both competitive and equitable. See each characteristic of a good job offer for more information about it.

To ensure that a job offer you design is competitive and equitable, you should seek input from your company's Human Resources Department.

From HR personnel, you can learn the average salaries and benefits for similar positions requiring similar experience in your company.

You can also check that your offer complies with your company's policy on employee pay and benefits.

Frank has interviewed and evaluated candidates for a project management position in his construction company. He has identified Angela as the most suitable candidate and now needs to develop a job offer.

Frank researches the external market and discovers that in his company's area and industry, project managers have average starting salaries of between $50,000 and $65,000. He also determines the benefits these employees are typically offered.

Frank then consults his company's HR Department.

Question

What questions should Frank ask the HR Department?

Options:

1. "What's the average salary for employees with similar experience in project management positions?"

2. "Does the package I've put together comply with company policy?"

3. "What's the average of all employees' salaries in our company?"

4. "What's the lowest annual salary I can legally offer?"

Answer:

Option 1: This option is correct. By finding out the average salary for employees in similar positions with similar experience, Frank can determine whether the offer he's thinking of making is equitable.

Option 2: This is a correct option. It's important for Frank to ensure the offer he makes complies with his company's employment policies. The HR Department can assist him in doing this.

Option 3: This option is incorrect. Knowing the average salary of all employees won't necessarily help Frank determine an offer that's equitable. A fair offer will depend on the type of position, experience of the candidate, and the responsibilities the candidate will be expected to fill.

Option 4: This is an incorrect option. The offer needs to be competitive – it must be designed to attract the selected candidate, rather than being as low as possible.

Frank decides to make his offer $60,000 per annum as a starting salary, plus benefits. He has ensured this offer is competitive and equitable, so now it's up to Angela to accept or reject this offer.

Making the offer

Before you speak to a candidate about an offer, you should put the offer in writing. Then, using exactly what's in the written offer, you should make the offer verbally.

This will help ensure you're clear and concise, and that you don't unintentionally promise a candidate more than you should.

A written offer should include these components:
- job title,
- department and reporting manager job requirements,
- schedule and location, and
- Salary.

Making an offer verbally helps you sell it. However, you should be careful to cover only what's on the written offer. Remember that what you say at this point forms a verbal contract. If you leave room for misinterpretation or imply your company agrees to something beyond what it's really offering, it could cause conflict later on.

When you're making the verbal offer, you should ask if the candidate has any questions. Sometimes a candidate will make a request.

If it's a small request, you may be able to resolve it during the conversation and then adjust your written offer. If it's a bigger request, for example related to salary or benefits, you should confer with your HR Department before changing anything.

Handling negotiations

The first request that Angela makes is fairly small. Frank can easily answer this request during their conversation on the phone. Most companies, including Frank's, have flexible work schedules.

The second request that Angela makes is one that requires consultation with the company's HR Department. This is because it may not be fair to give

Angela more money, relative to what employees in similar positions with similar experience are getting.

You update the written offer with all the approved changes. For example, you move the start date out by one week. Once the candidate signs and returns this offer, the employment contract is established.

Inform candidates

Once you've selected someone for a position, it's important that you let every other candidate who applied for the position know. Failing to do this could damage your company's reputation. It can also mean that unsuccessful candidates, some of whom possess valuable skills, may be less interested in applying for jobs at your company in the future, even when positions for which they're well suited become available.

It's perfectly acceptable to send written rejection letters to candidates who didn't make it through the resume screening process. For candidates who came in for a face-to-face interview, a verbal rejection is usually more appropriate. This is particularly the case for candidates who made it through to the final round of interviews.

See each type of rejection for more information about it.

Written rejection

When writing a letter of rejection, you should be respectful. To soften the blow, you might compliment the applicant in some way and go on to say you've found a candidate who fits the position better.

You can also retain the candidate's interest in your company by saying something along the lines of "We'll keep your resume on file and contact you if a suitable position becomes available."

A sample written rejection reads "Thank you for your interest in Gleeson Associates. We regret to inform you that we've appointed someone else to fill the position of project manager. While your resume is impressive, it didn't fit the exact profile needed for the position available at this time. We'll keep your resume on file and contact you if a suitable position becomes available.

Once again, thank you for your interest in Gleeson Associates."

Verbal rejection

Candidates you've met face-to-face should be told of your decision over the phone. This reflects better on you and your organization. Keep it simple by first asking if they have time for a brief conversation and then immediately get to the point of the call. Just tell the unsuccessful candidates you've found another candidate who is a better fit for the position. Then thank them for coming in for an interview. If you think there might be a possible fit in the future, you can say so, but try not to raise any false hopes.

Also avoid giving a specific reason for the rejection, because you don't want to be put in the position of defending your choice. The rejected candidates may be disappointed, angry, or hurt. You don't want to give them an opportunity to begin an argument with you.

Question

Which are effective strategies for making an offer to a candidate?

Options:

1. Ensure the offer is attractive in relation to those available from competitors and that it's fair, given what others in your company currently earn

2. Compose an offer in writing and use it as the basis for a verbal offer

3. Let all unsuccessful candidates know that you're appointing someone else

4. Speak directly to every unsuccessful candidate to inform them of your decision

5. Ensure you offer the candidate more than your company currently pays employees in similar positions

6. Make minor changes to the written offer during the verbal offer

Answer:

Option 1: This option is correct. The job offer you develop should be both competitive and equitable.

Option 2: This is a correct option. You should create an offer in writing and use this as the basis for a verbal offer you make to the successful candidate. Then, if the candidate agrees to accept the offer, immediately send this person the written version of the offer to sign.

Option 3: This option is correct. You need to notify all unsuccessful candidates of your decision, to keep your company's reputation intact.

Option 4: This is an incorrect option. It's perfectly acceptable to use letters to inform candidates you didn't meet face-to-face with. Candidates you did meet with should receive verbal rejections.

Option 5: This option is incorrect. Your offer should be competitive in relation to offers for similar positions in the external market – but it should be equitable in relation to what your company offers existing employees.

Option 6: This is a correct option. When you speak with the successful candidate, this person may want to make minor changes, such as those related to working hours. You can make these, but larger changes may require consultation with the HR Department.

You should use three strategies when making a job offer. First develop an offer that's competitive and equitable, and put this in writing. Then make a verbal offer to the candidate and follow this up with the written version of the offer. Finally, notify all unsuccessful candidates.

REFERENCES

References

- **Smart Hiring at the Next Level: The Complete Guide to Finding and Hiring the Best Employees** - 2005, Robert W. Wendover, Sourcebooks
- **The Evaluation Interview: How to Probe Deeply, Get Candid Answers, and Predict the Performance of Job Candidates, Fifth Edition** - 2002, Richard Fear and Robert Chiron, McGraw-Hill
- **Human Resources Kit For Dummies** - 1999, Max Messmer, John Wiley & Sons
- **Success for Hire: Simple Strategies to Find and Keep Outstanding Employees** - 2008, Alexandra Levit
- **Successful Interviewing and Recruitment** - 2008, Rob Yeung, Kogan Page
- **Smart Hiring at the Next Level: The Complete Guide to Finding and Hiring the**

- **Best Employees** - 2005, Robert W. Wendover, Sourcebooks, 9781402205897
- **The Evaluation Interview: How to Probe Deeply, Get Candid Answers, and Predict the Performance of Job Candidates, Fifth Edition** - 2002, Richard Fear and Robert Chiron, McGraw-Hill
- **Successful Interviewing** - 2000, Diane Arthur
- **Human Resources Kit For Dummies** - 1999, Max Messmer, John Wiley & Sons
- **Harvard Business Essentials: Hiring and Keeping the Best People** - 2002, Harvard Business School Publishing, Harvard Business Press
- **Recruiting, Interviewing, Selecting, and Orienting New Employees, Fourth Edition** - 2006, Diane Arthur
- **Interviewing and Selecting High Performers: A Practical Guide to Effective Hiring** - 1997, Larry Smalley, Richard Chang Associates
- **Perfect Phrases for Perfect Hiring: Hundreds of Ready-to-Use Phrases for Interviewing and Hiring the Best Employees** - 2007, Lori Davila and Margot King, McGraw-Hill
- **The Evaluation Interview: How to Probe Deeply, Get Candid Answers, and Predict the Performance of Job Candidates, Fifth Edition** - 2002, Richard Fear and Robert Chiron, McGraw-Hill

- **High-Impact Interview Questions** - 2006, Victoria A. Hoevemeyer
- **Recruiting, Interviewing, Selecting, and Orienting New Employees, Fourth Edition** - 2006, Diane Arthur
- **How to Compete in the War for Talent: A Guide to Hiring the Best** - 2001, Carol A. Hacker, DC Press
-

GLOSSARY

Glossary

A

analyze - The act of interpreting and understanding something.

B

behavioral-based interview - An interviewing style that involves working through a candidate's resume, asking questions where relevant based on what's in the resume.

behavioral-based questions - Questions regarding a candidate's behavior in a past, real situation.

biographical interviewing - An interview in which behavioral-based questions are asked to determine whether candidates have required competencies, based on how they dealt with relevant situations in the past.

C

candidate - A person who's being considered for a job.

close-ended question - A question that requires a short or single-word answer, such as "yes" or "no."

compare - The act of seeing how similar or different two or more things are to one other.

competency - A set of skills, attributes, or characteristics that equip a person to perform a specific task or job.

competency-based question - A question designed to determine whether someone has required competencies, based on how this person handled specific examples of situations or problems in the past.

competitive - Matching or exceeding what's available in the external market.

D

discrimination - When job candidates are asked questions relating to race, gender, religion, natural origin, disability, marital status, or sexual orientation, this is considered to be discrimination.

E

electronic resume screening software - Software that uses scanning and user-defined classification to store candidates' resumes in an electronic database.

employment legislation - Legislation governing the employment of staff.

equitable - Fair. In relation to job offers, an offer is equitable if it's fair in relation to what existing employees in a company are currently paid, given the responsibilities associated with the position being offered.

evaluate - The act of measuring something to see how good or bad it is.

H

hypothetical question - A question asking how someone would behave or respond, given a particular situation that could occur in the future.

I

interviewer - The person who leads an interview and asks the candidate questions.

J

job analysis - A process through which information about a job is gathered. This information is used to write the job description.

job description - A document that describes a job, usually to attract applicants. Its key elements include an overview, an outline of the reporting structure associated with the position, a list of tasks and responsibilities, and a list of required qualifications and skills.

L

leading question - A question that encourages the person asked to return a specific answer; it implies that only one answer is correct.

loaded question - Also called a multichoice question, a question that forces the person asked to choose from two or more specified alternatives, when the accurate answer isn't necessarily among these alternatives.

M

multichoice question - See loaded question.

N

nepotism - The practice of favoring family or friends in employment decisions.

O

open-ended question - A question that prompts a detailed response, which the person asked is free to structure in any way.

P
pre-employment testing - Testing that requires job candidates to undergo aptitude, psychological, and personality tests, as well as various medical and drug tests before employment.
probing question - A question designed to uncover further information – for example, about a response to a previous question.
Q
qualification - A recognition – such as a degree, diploma, certificate, or license – that a candidate has completed a course of study or test, or has acquired specific skills or knowledge.
R
red flag - In a resume, a worrying piece of information or an ambiguity that signals a potential problem with a candidate.
reporting structure - Within an organization, the people to whom an employee reports and whom that employee supervises.
responsibilities - The tasks and duties an employee is required to perform in the course of their job.
resume screening - A process of sifting through job applicants' resumes to identify the candidates worthy of further investigation through interviews.
S
situational question - A question, based on hypothetical behavior, that's used to gain insight into a candidate's anticipated behavior in a hypothetical situation.

Printed in Great Britain
by Amazon